MW01595160

Man to Man

Real Answers About Manhood

RICK JOHNSON
Author of *Wealth Is Possible* ©

Man to Man
Real Answers About Manhood

Cover Design © Copyright 2006
J. Benjamin Young, Sr.

First Printing April 2006

ISBN
0-9711876-2-2

VChase Investment Group, LLC
P.O. Box 4613
San, Dimas, CA 91773

Printed in the United States of America

A Division of
His Image Publishing, Inc.
P.O. Box 14311, Fremont, CA 94539-1211

Man to Man

Real Answers About Manhood

RICK JOHNSON

Author of *Wealth Is Possible* ©

DEDICATION

This book is dedicated to all
my future grandsons, great-grandsons
and so forth.
As I am writing this book
you are not born,
but I want to leave you with information
to become a better man
and help guide you through life.
Bless your children as I have blessed you.

I love you.

TABLE OF CONTENTS
"Man to Man, *Real Answers About Manhood*"

PREFACE

Man-to-Man is about empowering young men with information concerning manhood. It covers a host of topics that are short and packed with sound principles.

The right of passage for any young man regardless of race, creed, economic level etc, needs coaching. Since, we are not born as men; we need a roadmap to help guide us on this journey from boyhood to manhood. This roadmap must help us matriculate through manhood by teaching on money, relationship, marriage, dating, self-respect, fatherhood and leadership, to name a few. It is our prayer that Man-to-Man exposes and explores the information you need to become a man of quality.

The characters used in this book are all fictional. Names have been randomly chosen to provide a narrative approach on expressing a point.

This book is written for several reasons.
- To the single mom, who does not have the answers her tender boy is searching for and so desperately need.
- To the young man who has questions about his identity and sexuality who can glean valuable nuggets and not leave life to chance.
- To the young man, who through marriage must raise another man's child (ren).
- To the man who is surrounded by a host of wide-eyed young men, a resource he can give as a gift to those he cannot personally reach.

- To the man who's been thrust into fatherhood without an instruction manual can use this book as a resource kit for real answers.
- The list goes on.

Lastly, the purpose of this book is to make you think because we cannot control the way you act. If we can provide you with real answers, we can help minimize your mistakes. So, when you are in a compromising or confused situation, we pray something in this book will help you make better choices.

CHAPTER 1

Sex Isn't A Dirty Word

The Birds and the Bees

Once a week, Phillip and his father would sit on the back porch and talk about life. At sixteen, he was a very curious young man. One day while he and his father were talking about sports, Phillip decided to ask his father a question, "Dad, why have we never talked about the birds and the bees?"

His father responded, "Phillip would you like to talk about it now?"

Phillip said, "Yes."

Phillip's father explained, "The birds and the bees are about procreation."

"What is procreation?" Phillip asked with a puzzled look.

His father responded, "Procreation is when a man and wife come together during sex and eventually they have a baby. You see Phillip, sex is not a dirty word, but it is one of the most beautiful words in our vocabulary."

Phillip asked, "Is it wrong for a man to have feelings for a woman who's not his wife?"

"No, it is very natural. However, the bedchamber is a sanctuary that is pure and reserved for a husband and wife," his father replied. "Today, kids call it bumping and grinding. What they do not know is they are becoming one."

Phillip looked even more bewildered to his father's statement and asked, "What do you mean about becoming one?"

He replied, "Phillip let me draw you a picture. Every time a person has sex, they are tying or connecting themselves to the person. It is called a soul-tie. For example, if a young man has sex with 20 girls, each one of those girls will have a part of him."

Phillip replied, "Dad, I still do not understand what you mean about soul-tie."

"Let me put it this way. We are a spiritual being, housed in a physical body. Intimacy is the one thing that unites man and woman as one."

"I get it now."

"Son, I know that some would say what I am telling you is prehistoric, but with the old fashioned way, we never had the problems your generation is having concerning teen pregnancy nor sexually transmitted diseases.

"Today, sex is publicized everywhere. Your peer group is bombarded with sex showered everyday on T.V., radio, in print, and now the Internet, to name a few.

"Phillip, I cannot force you to abstain from sex. However I hope you will grow up and save yourself for marriage like I did."

Shocked, Phillip replied, "You mean that you and mom never had sex before marriage?"

"That's right. We had many opportunities, but never gave into our lusts."

Phillip asked, "How did you and mom keep from having sex because many of my friend's parents had kids before they got married?"

His father replied, "We did it out of love and respect for each other. We made a commitment that if we truly loved one another, we would wait.

"One more thing, being a man has nothing to do with keeping a sexual scorecard. Manhood is about having integrity, honesty, and being a positive example. By integrity, we mean having strong moral values in a society that is slowly slipping down the moral mountain. Honesty is telling the truth even when it hurts. Lastly, a positive example is being a trendsetter by doing what others will not, that is, respecting yourself and keeping your zipper up and pants on.

"Phillip, here are several things I did to help myself from crossing the line -

- Took cold showers. I know it sounds old, but it worked.
- Talked with a responsible adult about my sexual drive.
- Made a commitment to keep myself until marriage.
- Avoided dirty books, movies, and music.
- Stayed active with work or sports."

As the conversation ended, Phillip had a higher respect for his father and wished he could do the same. As Phillip grew up and went to college he remembered what his father taught him.

Although Phillip heard about the college parties, he never attended them. These parties were filled with drinking binges, drugs, and sex. Instead, Phillip and his girlfriend, Samantha, chose to play it safe and stay at the library. This worked well for the first year, but as their relationship grew, it became more difficult to resist their passion for one another.

On one occasion, Phillip's friend, Larry, asked if he wanted to join him at a dorm party. He told him no, that he would just study and then go to bed. But, about an hour into his studies, Samantha came to his dorm, needing help with her math project.

In the middle of their studies, they found themselves in deep passion on his bed. While overcome with passion, Phillip remembered what his father told him about soul-tie. At the thought, he jumped up and stopped everything.

Samantha asked, "What's wrong?"

He said, "I know this will sound crazy, but I respect you too much to violate our virginity. I made a commitment to myself that I would wait until marriage, and if I continue to kiss you like that, I know I will give in." So, they both got dressed and Phillip kept his promise and never had sex until he was married.

Man Point or Question:
What do you think about Phillip and his father's relationship?

Man Point or Question:
What do you think about his commitment to abstain from sex until marriage?

Man Point or Question:
What is your plan about your virginity?
(Or if you're not a virgin, your plan about your sexuality now?)

Man Point or Question:
Who can you talk to about sex?

The Myth About Sowing Your Oats

It was a Friday, Craig and Mercedes were at the movies. At the end of the movie, Craig decided to take Mercedes to the park under his favorite tree. They started kissing, and then Craig pulled off Mercedes' blouse, unhooked her bra and was moments from hitting a home run. The steam in the car was so thick anyone could cut it with a knife. Slowly, Craig's sinister approach was drawing him closer to his goal, sex.

This is what Craig had been waiting for... Mercedes began to unbutton her jeans and took them off as Craig was about to explode with anticipation. Nothing was going to stop him now because he was just minutes from showing Mercedes who's the man. As he looked at her naked body, his heart began to pound harder than a sledge hammer breaking concrete.

Just as Craig lay on top of her to conduct business, Mercedes said, "I do not want to get pregnant." He quickly replied, "Don't worry; I will not get you pregnant." Within minutes, Craig and Mercedes were engaged in sexual intercourse.

How did Craig learn about sex? He learned it from his friends. They talked about it on many occasions. After being overwhelmed with sexual conversation, he decided to give it a try without regard of contracting a disease or Mercedes getting pregnant.

After they finished their five-minute sexual encounter, it was time to get dressed and go home. Although Craig felt good, Mercedes didn't. She knew her dignity was gone. But, it didn't matter, Craig had sown his oats.

What did Craig do wrong? One, he showed lack of self control. It was very easy to give in to his sexual urges, but it takes strength to say no. Two, his respect was gone. Not only did Mercedes lose her respect, Craig lost his too. Mercedes realized that Craig did not have the personal strength to say no and protect her value. But who cares what she thinks? Craig got his, right?

Like many other foolish advice, sowing ones oats is a narrow view about being a man. The moment a person loses their virginity, they can never get it back. You may remember the testimony of the former basketball champion, A.C. Green, formerly of the Los Angeles Lakers. He was an excellent role model who kept his virginity throughout his entire career. He had access to any woman he wanted, but chose to remain a virgin and wait until marriage.

I knew of several young men that sowed their oats early in life and altered their history. One of them had seven kids from five different women. I have heard this young man is still struggling financially because most of his money goes to his kids.

Several others contracted AIDS and died without having the chance to enjoy life. They will never see their kids grow up nor play with their grand kids. They will never have the joy of watching their bride walk down the aisle and hearing the preacher say, "I present to you Mr. and Mrs. so and so." Yes, they had their fun, but today they are paying a heavy price for one or several bad decisions.

There are some who encourage you to explore your sexuality, but they are not telling you the whole story. You are receiving one-sided information and this can be very detrimental to your life. You do not have to do one thing written in this book, but you will have to pay the price for any wrongdoing and that price may be more than you want to pay.

Earlier, we gave you a scenario about a man going to the movies and then having sex under his favorite tree. Let me take it one step further. Whenever you have sex, at some point you will ejaculate. What is ejaculation? It is when semen or fluid is released from your body. To you, this may be the best feeling you have ever experienced. However that exchange of fluid can cause many problems.

So, you might think all you have to do is take it out before you ejaculate. Wrong. She can still be a candidate for getting pregnant. Just because you say she won't get pregnant doesn't mean she won't. Do not fool yourself, sex is very powerful. Also, exchanging fluid with your partner can pass on various diseases. For instance, today thousands of young people are getting the deadly disease, AIDS, from having sex.

What are some of the first signs of AIDS? Here are several examples downloaded from http://www.globalchange.com/ttaa/ttaa3.htm:

> "The first thing that happens after infection is that many people develop a flu-like illness. This may be severe enough to look like glandular fever with swollen glands in the neck and armpits, tiredness, fever and night sweats. Some of those white cells are dying, the virus is being released, and for the first time the body is working hard to make correct antibodies. At this stage the blood test will usually become positive as it picks up the tell-tale antibodies. This process of converting the blood from negative to positive is called 'sero-conversion'. Most people do not realize what is happening, although when they later develop AIDS they look back and remember it clearly. Most people have produced antibodies in about twelve weeks."

If you think you have contracted this deadly disease, do not think an over-the-counter medication such as aspirin will cure you; it will not. You need to inform your parents and have them make an appointment to see a doctor right away.

The more information you have the better choices you can make. You have one life to live and every decision you make has a lasting result.

Man Point or Question:
What changes should Craig make about his sexual life?

Man Point or Question:
What do you think are the dangers of sowing your oats?

Sex Is a Choice

One day Dwayne was home watching T.V. and the phone rang. Upon answering, he realized it was Tammy, a girl he had been fond of for some time. She told him hat she was on her way to his house and she would like to have sex with him. At that moment, Dwayne had a choice to stop every thing.

Instead of saying no, he gave an open invitation. He thought, "In ten minutes Tammy will be over. What am I going to do?"

But wait, he still has a choice to stop every thing before it starts.

Tammy knocks on the door and when he opens it, Tammy pulls open her jacket and the only thing she's wearing is her birthday clothes. What should Dwayne do? If he was like most, he would do what comes natural, the sex thing.

At that point he had several chances to stop this uncontrollable locomotive, but he made a choice not to. Why should he; she called him right? He was home watching T.V., plus what will his friends think if the word got out that he refused?

What could he have done to avoid this tragic event? Tell her no? It would not be the most popular choice, but it would be the most sensible. Now let's continue with the illustration.

As Dwayne looked at this vision of a perfect body, he knew he had to make a choice. First, he needed to get control of the situation. He asked if she would come in and have a seat. Tammy was somewhat confused because Dwayne did not seem interested in having sex.

She looked Dwayne in the eye and asked, "Do you not find my body attractive?"

He replied, "Yes."

Then Tammy asked, "If you do, why are we sitting down and not going to your bed room?"

Dwayne responded, "There is something I need to tell you..."

Tammy interrupted, "Are you gay?"

He replied, "No, I'm not gay."

Dwayne pulled out a piece of paper and handed it to her. Tammy asked, "What is this?"

Dwayne answered, "A virginity contract."

She responded, "Virginity contract, what is this?"

He explained that he and his parents had created a contract that he would not have sex until he was married.

Tammy said, "Is that ring on your finger a part of the contract?

Dwayne said, "Yes, this ring is a reminder that I have a virginity contract until my wedding day."

Tammy felt rather embarrassed, but Dwayne continued to explain more about his contract. After several minutes Dwayne excused himself and went to his bedroom and found some clothes for Tammy to put on.

While Tammy was changing in the restroom, she thought how Dwayne had character and strength to stand for what he believed. She felt safe and respected him for keeping the contract. While she was still in the restroom, Dwayne's parents came home and he explained everything that happened.

When Tammy walked out, she greeted them with a smile. Dwayne told Tammy that his parents knew everything. They all set down and Tammy began asking Dwayne's parents to help her with a virginity contract. As years went by, Tammy and Dwayne had a strong platonic relationship but eventually their passion turned into love and they got married.

Now that we have shared Dwayne's position on pre-marital sex, do you feel you have a choice to have sex or not? Of course you do. You have the right to do whatever you want, no matter what anyone says. It is your prerogative. But, having the prerogative doesn't make it right.

How can you make a wise decision about having sex or not? You might ask your parents, youth pastor or a respected adult to help you in the creation of a virginity contract. Even if you are not a virgin, you can renew your commitment to chastity.

What do you gain by fornicating (having sex outside of marriage)? You may receive the praise of your friends, but is it worth losing your self-respect or getting STD? No way! Regardless of what people think about you, it is your life and your choice to refrain from sex.

In reality, the only thing you gain is a few minutes of pleasure, but possibly a life of problems. It is not worth it! The one constant that you have is a choice, but you must use it wisely. Dwayne's contract gave him the strength to say no.

Man Point or Question:

What do you think about Dwayne's contract?

Man Point or Question:

What would you like to put in your virginity contract?

What Is Puberty?

At thirteen, Brad was a very energetic young man, friendly, bright, and very confident. He loved every sport but his favorite was football. He was known to be a stats buff and many of his friends knew he would grow up and become a football analysis.

One day while washing his face, Brad began to notice pimples. He did not take much thought of this until he awakened one day to find that the pimples had doubled. Each day Brad would see more pimples. One of his friends told him not to burst the pimples because it would leave marks. He did not mention this to his parents. Instead he tried various types of products, but without success. Brad did not know what was happening, but knew that whatever it was, he needed help.

One morning, Brad noticed that when he got out of the bed he had a teepee without a squaw. That is, he was hard without a girl being around. Brad did not want anyone to see his teepee, so he put on larger clothing before going to the restroom.

On another occasion, Brad started noticing hair in his pubic area and under his arms. Plus, he began having a strong body odor that was quite embarrassing in public. These body changes made him more self-conscience, which made him become depressed.

As time passed, Brad noticed his voice started to crack, his shoulders started to become broader and he began to get taller. These changes were well received because Brad liked the idea of becoming taller. Then the unthinkable happened.

One night, Brad was in a deep dream about a girl he liked and was awakened by a mysterious feeling. Upon awakening, he saw a strange creamy clear wet spot on his sheets. He jumped up and ran to the rest room. This was the ultimate shock to his ego; Brad had wet the bed and felt like a child. He had never wet his bed before. Why tonight? Brad did not know that he had just experience what is a called a wet dream. What is a wet dream? Simply, it is a discharge of creamy clear fluid called, 'semen' that occurs doing sleep.

How would Brad explain his wet dream to his parents? To avoid the whole encounter, he got up early in the morning, changed his sheets and placed them in the washer to cover any signs of what happened. Brad went back to his room and closed the door in complete confusion. He was experiencing physical transformation and did not know what to do.

Eventually Brad's father found out and talked to him about what he was experiencing. "Brad," his father said, "You do not have to be embarrassed or confused about your body changing. Every young man has gone through this experience. Your grandfather and I have gone through this transition in life. What you are experiencing is called puberty."

"Dad, what is Puberty?"

"Puberty is the period of time when young men begin to grow up and change in several areas. One, the body will feel like it is going haywire. Two, your mind might start thinking more about girls and less about your buddies.

"Thirdly, socially you may become aloof because of body changes and fear of rejection. This is normal and you should not be alarmed. No, you are not weird, you are normal and we congratulate you for this wonderful time of your life.

"Puberty is when young men transition into adolescence. What is adolescence? It is your internal clock saying it's time to leave childhood and start the journey of becoming a man. Adolescence does not make you a man, but you are on your way."

Brad said, "Dad I really felt confused and scared. Does every young man experience the same thing?"

"No son, every young man is different concerning puberty. Some teenagers start sooner than others and some young men experience puberty longer then others. There is no order in which things will happen, but here are some signs you might experience in your teenage years:

1. Puberty could happen between ages 12 – 17
2. Can last up to six years
2. Acne or bumps on your face
3. Growth spurt
4. Widening of shoulders
5. Voice change (deepening)
6. Growth of genital hair
7. Muscle changes (stronger)
8. Wet dreams
9. Spontaneous erection
10. Desire for sex

In closing, puberty is a time when young men start desiring sex. Your hormones may be off the chart and you might not be able to control how you feel. When girls come around, you might even have an erection. My mother knew I was interested in girls because I started taking baths in the middle of the day, ironing my clothes, and wearing my brother's cologne.

Man Point or Question:
What do you think about Craig's changes?

Man Point or Question:
Are you experiencing puberty? If so, how are you handling it?

Man Point or Question:
Who can you talk to about your puberty experience?

Teen Fatherhood

Each year thousands of young men become teen fathers. At first it may seem exciting, but after the child is born, the fun stops and the real world begin. When a young man becomes a father, he is faced with tough decisions. In the early story, "The Myth About Sowing Your Oats", we shared the story of Craig and Mercedes. Let's rejoin their sexual adventure.

One day Craig was at the park playing basketball with his buddies when Mercedes and her parents drove up. Mercedes got out of the car and told Craig she needed to talk to him and after a couple of minutes he got in the car and they drove to his house.

When they got to the house, Craig still did not have a clue of what was going on. They walked in the house and sat down at the table with Craig's parents and Mercedes' parents. Mercedes' father looked at her and told her to talk. She looked at Craig with tears in her eyes and said, "Remember, I told you not to get me pregnant?"

He replied, "Yes."

"You did not keep your promise. I am pregnant with your child." Mercedes words were like a knife slicing across his heart.

The atmosphere in the room was very heavy. Both mothers began to cry and caress one another. Mercedes' father could only look at Craig with a cool stare while watching his wife and daughter cry. However, Craig's father did not say a word but had a vacuous look on his face.

Craig had high educational goals. He had planned to attend the local university, then law school. He always dreamt of being an attorney and working on Wall Street. Like Craig, Mercedes had high educational goals. She was a 4.0 student on the road of becoming a brain surgeon. Neither one of them planned on being a teen parent. How could one night turn into such a tragedy? After thirty minutes, Mercedes and her parents left and Craig and his parent sat there quietly for a moment in shock and disbelief.

Then his father asked, "Is this your child?" He said that many of the guys in the neighborhood said Mercedes was known to be with other boys. His mother said, "Do not bring shame to our house by denying this child if it is yours." Then his father said, "What were you thinking? If this is your child, how are you going to take care of it?"

At seventeen years of age, Craig had no means of taking care of a child. He did not have a job or any savings. Like so many, he never planned on getting a girl pregnant by just having a few moments of fun- sex. He followed every step down like his friends told him, even to pulling it out just in time. He thought, "How could this happen to me, I did every thing right?" Craig could not see his future and how he could be a father at such a young age. Craig was only a few months away before he left for college and now he had become a teen father.

Craig never counted on his father's rejection. His father told him that he would not pay for his college and he had to get a job and take care of his child. Craig had seen his father's rejection, but this wasn't like before. His father's rejection was not for not taking out the trash when instructed or not cleaning his room. None of those compared to the consequences of becoming a father.

As Craig walked upstairs he thought that becoming a father was like going down with the Titanic. His life was over before even getting started.

There are thousands of Craigs on this earth. They come in packages of Black, White, Latino, Chinese, and Korean to name a few; race does not matter. Some of them are rich, others middle class or poor. Teen pregnancy is not prejudice nor is it ever planned.

Everyone in the family suffers as a result of teen parenting. In spite of how Craig's father felt, he was placed at a crossroads of helping or not helping his son. His mother must now plan on watching their grandchild and sacrifice many of her dreams to help her son. Mercedes' parents will have to rearrange their home to accommodate their grandchild.

Craig and Mercedes both have to make decisions about going to college or getting jobs. As a result of their one action, both Craig and Mercedes now realized how their selfish act created a domino effect and hurt people other than themselves.

Later that night, Craig's father came upstairs to comfort him. "Son, I want to apologize for coming at you so strong."

"No dad, I made the decision to have sex on my own and now my life has been changed."

"Yes Craig, your life has changed, but you can still turn and make some good out of this. Son, when a young man becomes a teen father, he is faced with an uphill battle. Here is what my father taught me to expect if I got a girl pregnant:

- It's hard to envision future achievements because of fatherly duties
- Emotional struggle of being a young man and a father at the same time
- Possible fight of custody and/or visiting rights
- Possible rejection from member of my family

"Craig, I have failed you. Maybe if I had talked to you, this might not have happened. If this is your child, I will stand by your side every step of the way."

Man Point or Question:
What do you think about Craig and Mercedes' situation?

Man Point or Question:
What do you think about teen pregnancy?

Man Point or Question:
Are you sexually active like Craig and are you prepared to become a teen father?

Man Point or Question:
What are you doing to protect your virginity until marriage?

What Is Safe Sex?

There is a great debate today about safe sex. One side says safe sex is abstinence, while the other side says it's okay as long as no one gets diseases. If you take the position of abstinence you remove all risk. However, if you agree with the second position, than you must place your trust in the reliability of condoms or other conventional methods of protection. Let's see how Jared addressed what he learned about safe sex.

Jared heard many people talk about safe sex. As a fifteen year old virgin, he was very curious about his sexuality. One day his school had a safe sex workshop so he decided to attend. During the workshop, a speaker told the kids that condoms were safe. Although this information seemed okay, Jared decided to seek more information before taking his first step.

He searched online and found many websites echoed the speaker's position. He talked with several friends and they gave him the same advice. Jared talked to his parents and unlike everyone else they did not believe in the use of condoms for safe sex. They told him no sex is safe sex.

One day Jared heard that there was going to be a private party and his friend asked if he wanted to go because all the fine girls were going to be there. Jared decided to go. When he got to the party, it was like his friend said, there were girls everywhere.

Jared heard people talking about the dark room so he decided to check it out. When he entered the room he saw outrageous sex in full swing. There were girls with girls, boys with girls and boys with boys. As he entered the room, there was a punch bowl next to the door with condoms in it. Jared did not want to be left out so he took a condom and joined in the "fun".

The next day, the news of the party was all over the school. The kids that did not attend asked about it, but no one would say anything. This party was exclusive, only for the in-crowd.

After a while, Jared's conscience began to bother him. At that point he decided that he would never participate in sex again until he got married. He wished he had listened to his parents' advice, but it was too late. However, he chose to make a vow to renew his virginity.

About a year later Jared's mother began to notice he had flu like symptoms and no matter what she tried, he never got better. So, she took him to the hospital for a check up. The doctor ran tests and said he would call when the tests came back. After several weeks the doctor's secretary called to schedule a meeting with Jared and his parents.

When Jared and his parents sat down, his mother could sense that something was wrong. The doctor looked at Jared and asked if he was sexually active and he said, "No." The doctor replied, "Jared, come clean with your parents." His mother asked, "Jared what have you done?" Again he said, "Nothing."

Losing patience and becoming tired with Jared's denial, the doctor said, "What I'm about to say is very difficult, but the flu like symptoms Jared has been experiencing are the result of a virus which causes AIDS."

After several minutes, Jared told his parents that a year ago he attended a party and tried sex with multiple partners. But since then he made a personal vow that he would never do it again.

His parents were in complete shock because they had no idea Jared had been involved in such things. Eventually in time Jared died of a complication of HIV.

Jared was a young man misguided about the topic of sex. He did not understand that condoms are only effective if it stays on and do not break. His one mistake cost him his life, but his story isn't new.

Many young kids and adults have put their trust in condoms only to find out that abstinence is the only true safe sex. Every time you have sex, you are committing to an aleatory trust between condoms and its ability to protect you. Are you willing to roll the dice for a few minutes of sexual fun? Ask yourself, is it worth the risk? There's no love in dying an unnecessary death.

Man Point or Question:
What do you think about Jared's tragic life?

Man Point or Question:
Do you believe condoms are safe? If yes, Why? If no, Why not?

Man Point or Question:
What do you think about the advice Jared received?

The Truth about Pornography

There is an explosion of teens searching the Internet for pornography. Many of the kids are searching for quick fun while others are taking it to other levels. As a society, we have been programmed by commercials with the thought of selling products, when in fact it is not just the product being sold, but sex.

George loved going to the park after school to meet up with his friends. One day, one of his friends, nicknamed Baby Joe, brought a paper bag and told everyone he had a special surprise in it. Like most young men, everyone wanted to know what was in the bag. After several minutes of taunting his friends, Baby Joe pulled out books of naked women. The "oohs" and "ahs" that ping-ponged back and forth was a sign that everyone enjoyed the pictures.

The boys looked forward to the third Thursday of every month in expectation of what new books Baby Joe would bring. For instance, one month he brought books on blondes, on another occasion brunettes. These private meetings went on for about a year under the radar of their parents.

George decided that the books were not enough and started searching late nights on the Internet for porn sites. He traveled from site to site searching for the next sexual high. Unlike the books, he now had access to thousands of pictures at his disposal. George could not keep this goldmine to himself, so he e-mailed his friends each site he visited.

By seventeen, George's addiction to pornography cost him more than $2,000 from his personal savings account. One day his mother asked about the missing money and George responded that he was using the money for a school project and it would be refunded to him later. Each night before going to bed he would log-in to various sites.

George was very good at covering his tracks from his parents. He maintained a good GPA, kept his room clean, and his chores done. To his parents, he was the model kid. But behind his dungeon door, George had a deadly secret slowing carving away his values.

Like George, each of his friends were depleting their funds. One by one, the boys were being intoxicated with this trash. For instance, Harry sold his motorcycle just to pay his online pornography account. Unfortunately, they had tapped into a cesspool of filth and they did not have the power to stop.

One Thursday, the boys were in the park talking about the various sites. It was starting to get dark and there was no one in the park except a girl out for jog. Baby Joe said, "Let's ask the girl to have sex." They all agreed except George. He decided that was his curtain call to go home.

As the group approached the girl, she could sense the boys were up to something wrong so she started running faster. She accidentally stepped into a hole and fell to the ground. Harry grabbed her and one by one, they raped her. After the rape, Baby Joe threatened to kill her if she said anything.

When George got home, he ran straight to his room and slammed the door shut. He felt bad about saying no, but George knew what his parents had taught him about hurting others. His parents hearing the sound of the door close, got up and knocked on the door, but George refused to open.

The next morning, the park rape made front page on the local newspaper. It was all over town that a gang of thugs had rapped the chief of police's daughter and she had identified one of them.

At breakfast, George's father asked what he thought about the story and George responded, "Who can believe what they put in the paper?" His father asked if he knew any kids that would do such a thing to an innocent girl. Before he could finish his sentence, the phone rang. It was the Chief of Police.

George's heart began racing as he listened to his father's responses on the phone. When his father got off the phone, he asked George if he ever heard of a guy named Baby Joe. He replied, "No." Why was his father asking so many questions? Well, he was the District Attorney. George finished his breakfast and left for school.

Within in an hour, Baby Joe was arrested and sung like a bird, telling the names of his rape buddies. A host of police went to the school and arrested everyone. Each boy was tried as an adult and received 20 years in state prison.

George made a bad decision about getting involved with pornography. However, he made a great choice by saying no to rape. He could have followed his friends, but instead of being in jail, he had a second chance.

As you read this story, you might think this could never happen to you. History has proven that pornography is a bad influence. Ted Bundy was a perfect example of how as a teen he used pornography and eventually became a serial killer. As the sickness of pornography continues, there will be more Ted Bundys being developed. What happened to George could happen to anyone that is addicted to the filth of pornography.

What should you know about pornography?
- One will eventually have to act out their fantasy
- It will eventually escalate to worse things
- It will alter your mindset
- It is very addictive

Man Point or Question:
What do you think about George's choice of friends?

Man Point or Question:
What do you think about the effects of pornography?

Man Point or Question:
What could George have done to stop things from going bad to worse?

Leave a Legacy Not a Seed

The rise of fatherless children has become an epidemic. Why are so many fathers abandoning their parental responsibility? This is too big of a question for a flippant response, but Matt will help us understand this question much clearer.

Matt was quite the ladies man. As a nineteen-year-old college student he considered himself a 21st Century Don Juan. Most of his romances lasted no more than one night. To him, any relationship that went pass one-night could end up tragically like his parents' relationship.

Matt was born while both of his parents were in high school. After much family pressure they decided to get married. Their marriage lasted for two years and ended when his father deserted him and his mother. As a result, Matt grew up bitter and vowed never to get married.

One day Matt was in line at the school cafeteria. He saw this girl named Julie sitting down by herself. Like before, he looked at women as if they had meat around their neck and he had just come off a forty-day fast. Matt walked up to Julie and asked if he could sit down and she said, "Yes." After his smooth talking, she agreed to go out on a date with him.

Unlike before, Matt found it difficult to get Julie to have sex with him. He tried everything in the book, but nothing seemed to work. She wasn't like the rest of the girls he had sweet talked into sex. Julie was different.

This began to bother Matt, so he went back to his playbook and decided to try a trick play. This time he would do something he had never done before. Matt changed his approach from bold and direct to the sensitive guy. It worked, she gave in and he added another point on his sex chart.

After their sexual encounter, Matt wanted to move on but Julie was determined not to let that happen. She called, sent cards but he never responded. To Matt, a couple more days of ignoring her and she would go away. Finally it worked; she got the message that Matt did not want a relationship.

After two months of non-contact, Matt received a letter from her. When he opened the letter Julie informed him that she was pregnant. Matt was determined not to repeat the cycle of his parents; he had to do something. He contacted Julie and scheduled a day to talk things over and she agreed.

As they began to talk, Matt noticed that Julie's eyes were teary. But being the heartless guy he was, he asked her how she knew it was his. She told him that he was the first and that was the only time she ever had sex.

Then he asked her if she would have an abortion. Julie adamantly replied, "I will not make two mistakes. I will not take the life of an innocent child for what I did. I accept the responsibility of becoming a mother and will give my child a chance like my parents did for me."

In his anger Matt said, "What do you want me to do, quit school, get and job and marry you?"

She said, "I never asked you for any thing. I only wanted you to know what happened. After you did not return my messages, I understood that you were a heartless person out for a one-night-stand. I cannot blame you for what I agreed to, you are what you are." Matt was shocked because no one had ever talked to him like that before. At the end of their talk, they went their separate ways.

Later that night, Matt sat down and thought about how he felt when his father left him and his mother. His so called father, whom Matt labeled a sperm donor, never attended one of his baseball games. He remembered hearing some of the kids' fathers shout, 'that's my boy.' No one said that about him.

He never had the experience of a father-son day at school like most of his friends. When father and son day would come, Matt kept it to himself. On one occasion, several of his friends asked about his father and he told them he was out of town.

He said this to avoid the embarrassing truth that he did not know his whereabouts. Locked in the caverns of his heart was anger and resentment towards the man that called himself a father.

Matt never even had a chance to attend a back-to-school night. He recalled the long hours his mother worked just to take care of the two of them. She worked from 8:00a.m. to 3:00p.m., came home for a short break and then went to her second job until midnight. It wasn't uncommon for Matt not to see his mother for three days at a time. Matt's father was no where to be found.

As a child, he broke his arm and remembered how his mother left her job, just to take him to the hospital. She stayed up late nights and held him until he went to sleep. Although he got so much love from his mother, he would always question why his father wasn't there.

At Matt's prom, his mother put together the biggest party she knew how. She had the table set up with the best food her money could buy. There were streamers and balloons throughout the house. She surprised Matt by arranging for many of her family members to be present. Also, she worked over time on the weekend just to pay for his tux and reserve a limo.

At his high school graduation, Matt remembered the smile on her face when his name was called. Matt was the first in his family to graduate high school and he knew she was very proud of him. After his rerun of thoughts, Matt made a commitment that his child would have a loving father.

The next day, Matt found Julie and took her aside to talk. As he looked into her eyes he thought that if he abandoned her, he would only repeat what happened to him and his mother. He shared his life experiences with Julie and explained why he treated her with such harshness. Matt mustarded everything he had and apologized for getting her pregnant. Julie asked, "What are we going to do?"

He explained that his parents were in the same situation and caved into the pressure and got married. He was afraid that history would repeat itself if they did the same. Julie agreed. Matt promised that when the baby was due she would not be alone. Also, he said they should both finish their education and offer their child a better chance.

Although Matt and Julie never got married, he kept his promise and helped raised their child, Matt Jr. He never missed a game, school project, birthday party, Christmas or a father-son event. Matt became the father to his son that he never had for himself.

Man Point or Question:
How do you feel about Matt's father?

Man Point or Question:
What do you think about Matt and Julie's choice concerning their child?

Man Point or Question:
How do you feel about men that abandon their children?

Chapter 2

Money, Money, Money

Smart Men Invest

Does money really make the world go 'round? The one thing we can count on for sure is money answereth all things. No matter who you are, you need money to live on this earth. As a man, people will judge you on how much you have in your bank account. Larry Taylor, better known to his friends as LT, will share how we learn about money.

LT had never learned how to handle money from his parents. They constantly talked about how broke they were. His dad's famous quote, "Money doesn't grow on trees!" In spite of all that negativity, LT was determined not to be broke like his parents.

Mr. Taylor, LT's father owned a consulting business while his mother worked as a nurse. Both of them made good money, but still lived paycheck-to-paycheck. His dad worked long hours and never had much time to spend with him. Although his mother was around she was too busy cooking and cleaning to stop and talk to LT.

One day LT decided to go around the corner and talk with Mr. Daniels. Many of the neighbors would say that he was an old rich and stingy man. LT walked up to the yard and saw Mr. Daniels sitting in his lawn chair. As he walked up, Mr. Daniels said, "Hello LT."

He replied, "How are you doing, Mr. Daniels?"

"Fine, if I can get this old body to work right. So how can I help you LT?"

LT said, "Mr. Daniels, I am tried of hearing people say how broke they are. What can you teach me about money?"

"Now that's a big question. So do you want me to be your mentor?" asked, Mr. Daniels.

"What's a mentor?" LT asked with a bit of curiosity.

"Well LT, a mentor is someone who teaches another person what he or she knows about a given subject. So you are asking me to be your financial mentor."

LT said, "Yes, I want you to be my financial mentor."

LT started with a question, "Why do the neighbors call you rich and stingy?"

Mr. Daniels started to laugh. Then he said, "LT, I am going to let you in on a secret about money. I will give you ten lessons. After you have completed one step we will move on to the next." LT agreed and gave him his full attention.

He asked a question, "When you look in the driveways of your neighbors, what do you see?"

"I guess cars," replied LT.

"Yes, but you're missing an important point, they are high priced cars. Most of the people around here buy pricey cars, work long hours to pay for these cars, but are too busy to enjoy them. So here is point number one, respect your money. A man must think about his future and not part with his money that easy. The neighbors think I am stingy, but in fact, they are selfish.

"What do you mean?" asked LT.

"Let me put in a way you might understand," replied Mr. Daniels.

"For instance, our neighbors drive pricey toys like Mercedes, BMWs, Lexus, and live in upscale homes. But who really owns those toys?"

LT interjected, "Is it wrong to have nice things?"

"Of course not," said Mr. Daniels. "The problem is buying all these toys and struggling to pay for them." Then LT said, "I thought everyone in the neighborhood owned their home."

"Not really LT," said Mr. Daniels. "The bank owns the mortgage until it is paid off."

"What's a mortgage?" asked LT.

Mr. Daniels said, "I'm glad you asked. LT, it is time you put on your thinking cap. A mortgage is a debt instrument or what you may have heard your parents call a loan."

"Yes, I heard them say that our home loan was too high, but I did not have a clue what they were talking about. Now I understand."

"That's right LT," responded Mr. Daniels. "Since the bank owns the mortgage, they own the house until the note or loan is paid in full. Another word for a loan is a long-term liability. That is, a loan that is not due within the first twelve months. The average home in this neighborhood has a thirty year loan attached to it."

"Thirty years? That is a long time to pay someone to live in their home," said LT.

"That's right, LT; boy are you catching on quickly," said Mr. Daniels. "Just remember LT, whenever you borrow someone's money, they own you until the bill is paid."

Mr. Daniels continued by saying, "For now I will give you two ways a home owner can pay off their loan early and save a lot of money."

"How can they do that?" replied LT.

Mr. Daniels said, "Let me explain: One, they can make one extra payment a year. For example, a homeowner has to make loan payment every month that adds up to twelve payments in a year. At the end of the year, a homeowner can make an extra or a thirteenth payment to their loan. In other words, they can make thirteen payments instead of twelve.

"Two, make bi-monthly payments or make two payments in a month instead of one, this will save them money. As an illustration, if a homeowner mortgage payment was $4,000 per month, they could pay $2,000 every other week. Now let me make one more point before I go into the house. Have you ever heard of interest, LT?"

"No," replied LT.

Then Mr. Daniels said, "Interest is a fee that a bank charges to borrow their money. For instance, if a person borrowed $100 dollars from you, you can charge a fee or interest for the use your money, such as $15.00. Therefore, when the borrower pays you back, you will receive the $100, also called the principle plus the $15.00 or interest."

With his eyes wide open, LT asked, "Are you saying I can lend someone money and charge them for using my money?"

"That's right," said Mr. Daniels. "Banks do it all the time. Well LT, I am finished and it's time for me to go in the house. Let's meet every Saturday at 9:00 a.m. and we will talk some more. Next time we meet, make sure you bring some flash cards on which to write your notes."

Man Point or Question:
What do you think about LT and Mr. Daniels' conversation?

Man Point or Question:
What do you know about money?

Man Point or Question:
How can you use Mr. Daniels' information about money?

How to Save Your Money

On Saturday morning LT got up early and went over to Mr. Daniels' house. When he came near the house he saw Mr. Daniels sitting in the lawn chair waiting. "Good Morning, Mr. Daniels." "Good morning to you, young man. Are you ready for your second lesson?" LT's smile was all he needed to know he was ready to learn more about money.

Mr. Daniels asked, "Do you remember our first lesson?" With excitement Daniel pulled out his flash cards and one by one he said, "We talked about mortgages, loans, pricey cars, and interest." "Great job; but what did you learn? LT paused for a moment then said, "I guess we should watch how much money we spend."

Mr. Daniels said, "Good answer. But, the one thing I want you to learn is not how much a person spends, but how much they have saved and invested. You see LT, our neighbors are good people but they spend more money than they save."

"Why is that important?" asked LT.

Leaning forward, Mr. Daniels took a deep breath and said, "If a person will not save, they will always struggle financially."

"So, how much should a person save?"

"Now you are thinking. Let's start with checking accounts. LT, when you start making money and open a checking account, make sure you get one that is free. This is very important. You can open a checking account with as little as $100 dollars. But, make sure it is free for you, no monthly fees. Just by getting a free checking account, you could save hundreds of dollars over time."

"Why will someone need a checking account?" asked LT.

"Another great question. Checking accounts help a person create a paper trail and spending habits." LT's blank look gave away he did not understand the words 'spending habits'.

So he continued, "LT have you ever heard of the words 'spending habits'?"

"No," answered LT.

Mr. Daniels explained, "Spending habits is how a person spends their money or what they value first. Question: Do you take your lunch or buy at school?"

"Most of the time I buy lunch."

"Ok, how much does it cost?"

"I guess $3.00."

"Then one of your spending habits is buying lunch instead of saving your money by taking a lunch from home."

"What's wrong with that?" asked LT.

"Nothing if a person is not interested in a better life," answered Mr. Daniels. However, if you have dreams of doing better, taking your lunch will save you a lot of money. In fact, I bought my first car with my lunch money."

"How did you do that?"

"I saved my lunch money by taking a bag lunch. When I had enough, I bought a lawnmower, cut lawns, saved my money and purchased my car."

"It sounds like you bought your car in steps."

Mr. Daniels looked at him and asked, "Are you sure no one has ever taught you about money?"

LT chuckled for a moment and then said, "No."

Mr. Daniels sensing LT's excitement said, "Many of the financial problems adults struggled with were developed from childhood? Take the example of the buying lunch instead of taking a paper bag lunch to school. Adults will get a loan on a car instead of saving their money and buying the car with cash."

LT threw his hands in the air with excitement and shouted, "I got it; a bank charges adults for using the bank's money!"

"You are definitely in the zone. Let me ask you a question. Do your parents have credit cards?"

"Yes, a lot of them," LT said.

"Credit cards are good, but when people pay their bills late the credit card companies charge a very high fee for being late."

"Are you talking about interest?" LT asked.

"Yes, also late fees. If a person would just pay the entire bill at the end of the month, they would avoid late fees and interest payments. Let me share one more savings strategy: Many adults do not have a savings strategy. Instead of saving a portion of their salary, they spend their money on things that take money from them. When you start working, make sure you save at least fifteen percent of your money every time you get paid. This requires a lot of self-discipline, but in the end, you will appreciate what it will do for you. It's time for me to go into the house. Next week I will share what you can do with the money you save."

Man Point or Question:
What have you learned about saving?

Man Point or Question:
What information have you gained from Mr. Daniels' information about saving?

Man Point or Question:
How are you currently saving your money?

You Don't Have To Be A Rocket Scientist to Make Money!

During the entire week, LT took a bag lunch to school. He also decided not to take the afternoon break to the vending machine with the guys. One of his friends asked, "LT, what's wrong with you, have you gone cheap on us?" LT was surprised his friends took such notice in his new spending habits.

He started to understand what Mr. Daniels was talking about. Before learning about money, LT would spend like everyone else. He bought lunch daily, purchased snacks from the vending machine and went to the donut shop after school. Now that he changed his spending habits, LT had saved $25.00.

The day of LT's next appointment with Mr. Daniels, as he approached the house, as before, Mr. Daniels was sitting in the lawn chair waiting. He could not wait to tell his mentor what happened at school. When LT sat down, Mr. Daniels asked, "How much money did you save this week?"

He looked at him in amazement and responded, "How did you know that I saved?"

"Well, you did save money this week, didn't you?"

"Yes, I saved $25.00."

"Give yourself two points. You are off to a good start! Don't worry about your friends because the more I tell you about money, the more they will not understand what you are doing.

"You see LT; this is why many of our neighbors call me stingy. I do not spend my money like they do. For instance, I never buy new cars, only used. My cars are no more than two to three years old when I purchase them. Plus, I buy wholesale and get the lowest price. Everyday, I am trying to save money so I can invest.

"Naturally, people are prejudiced against anything different. When your spending habits changed, your friends took it personal, made jokes, and treated you like you had betrayed them. Why? You chose to do something different and they felt threatened by your decision.

"The more you learn about money, the more your friends will feel you are rejecting them. You cannot please everyone and move forward in life. Now, let's talk more about investing. Have you ever heard of CDs?"

LT said, "No."

"No problem. One investment tool you might consider is CDs or Certificate of Deposits. For instance, a CD can be purchased from a bank, for a fixed amount of time and money. You can purchase it for six months, one, two, or three years, etc. Unlike a savings account, A CD will pay you a little more than a regular saving account.

"Here's how it works. You purchase a CD for $5,000. The bank holds your money in an account and pays you interest. Unlike a savings account, you cannot take money out until the maturity or expiration date."

LT liked the idea of getting paid interest. "Are you saying the bank will pay me interest like our neighbors are paying interest on their home loan?"

"That's right LT. Also, a CD is low risk, so you do not have to worry about losing your money like other investments." Mr. Daniels saw a different look on LT's face unlike before so he asked "What are you thinking about?"

He said, "Now I get it! You want me to save my money so I can invest it in things like CDs that will pay me interest, is that right?"

"That's correct LT. What I am teaching you will change your spending habits, but make you money. As I said before, many spending habits adults have bad or good start at a young age and develop into bigger habits over time. Okay, here is another tool. Have you ever heard about mutual funds?"

"No."

"Mutual funds are a tool that allows investor to diversify their portfolio. Now I know you might be thinking, 'what did he just say?' Here is a simplified version of diversification. To diversify means not to put all your money in one bag. Why? If that bag gets a hole in it, everything will eventually fall out. Question: Do you have a family portfolio?"

LT answered, "Yes."

"And in your family portfolio, do you have a lot of different pictures of you, your family, friends, etc.?"

"Yes, it has a lot of different pictures."

"Now use that same concept with a financial portfolio. It is an instrument used to hold different types of investments."

LT summarized, "So, saving my money lets me buy different types of investments. After purchasing an investment, they are put inside of my financial portfolio. And, my investments should be diversified so they will not fall out of the bag."

Mr. Daniels was bubbling with joy as he listened to LT. "That is right. Diversifying helps reduce your risk of losing everything. In other words, if one bag gets a hole in it, only the things contained in the bag will fall out. Your other bags will still be okay. Diversifying is what wise investors use everyday to protect their money.

"LT, the goal of a mutual fund is to make a profit. And an investor has to used seed capital or money, to help it grow. Are you getting this LT?"

LT nodded his head with a yes but Mr. Daniels knew he needed an example to help make his point.

"LT, seed capital works like this. The more money you put in the bag, the bigger the bag gets. When the bag becomes too big, you buy a bigger bag. That is, bigger investments."

This time LT smiled and said, "I got the picture."

"Good, but I want you to understand that investing can be risky. Many people have lost a lot of money investing."

"Have you ever lost any money?"

"Yes, many times. But I never stop investing because in the long run, I will make more money than I will lose. So it is worth the risk. LT, have you ever played chess?"

"Yes."

"Good, making money is like playing chess. One must first know the moves of each player. They must think long-term, that is five moves ahead. Lastly, each move is set up for one purpose that is to checkmate their opponent. Like chess, you must first learn what tools you can use to make money. Next, you will need to know how your investment tools can be moved. To be a wise investor, think long term. By long term I mean think five or ten years down the road, not just today.

"Earlier we talked about your school vending machine. The vending machine takes your money, but will make money for the investor that used their seed capital to buy it. One day you will have to put up seed capital to buy your own money making tool."

LT asked, "What can I invest my $25.00 in and make money?"

Mr. Daniels broke out in a loud laugh, but LT did not understand. He said, "I'm sorry for laughing but it was a happy laugh. It gives me joy to know that your mind is starting to connect the dots. Well, class is over and I will see you in two weeks."

LT asked, "Two weeks?"

"Yes, next week I will be out of town taking care of business." With those closing words LT went home.

Man Point or Question:
What do you remember about Mutual Funds?

Man Point or Question:
What is diversification?

Man Point or Question:
How are you going to build your financial portfolio?

The Money Playbook

After two weeks, LT was ready for his weekly financial meeting. As he came around the corner he was happy to see that Mr. Daniels was back in town. "How was your trip?"

"It was very nice," replied Mr. Daniels. "I brought you back a gift. This is a very important pen you will need one day, so take very good care of it."

"Thank you so much. Before we start, I want you to know something. For the last couple of weeks many of my friends have been asking me what we've been talking about. I haven't told anyone, but they are starting to call me stingy."

"Don't worry about it LT. Like I said before, people do not like change. Today I will start the ball rolling with the topic of how to leverage your money. By leveraging I mean using a small amount of money to control a large amount of property. Do you like football?"

LT's eyes opened wider than the Grand Canyon and he responded with a sound as if his team had just won the Super bowl, "Yes!"

"In football, every team has a playbook. That playbook has standard and trick plays. Correct?"

"Yes."

"Well, the financial playbook has some veers, shotgun and trick plays to name a few. Let's talk about the financial playbook concerning the vending machine to illustrate the point. What happens when you put your money in the vending machine?"

"I'm not sure where it goes, but I get a snack."

"Have you ever thought about where the money goes?"

"Not really."

"You are not alone. Most people are only interested in getting their snack or what we call instant gratification. That is, they have the 'give it to me right now' mentality. LT, that vending machine did not just show up at the school by accident. Plus you can bet the owner has one in every school in the district. Those machines cost several thousands but it makes the owner a lot of money."

LT asked, "Are you saying the owner uses his money to buy the vending machine; and, when he or she has enough money; they go out and buy more machines? That's leveraging your money?"

"That is correct."

"That's makes me rather mad," LT responded.

"Why is that?"

"For years I have be using that machine and now you are telling me the owner is getting rich off of me."

"I'm sorry to say it, but you're right. However, I am also giving you information so you can learn to do the same when you get older. Did you know that if you saved your money, bought a house, you could leverage your savings to make more money?"

"Yeah right, where am I going to by a house with $25.00?"

"While in college, one of my classmates took his student loan, leveraged it, and bought an apartment building. Today, he owns most of the property downtown. Another friend used this playbook and taught his son how to go for the bomb by helping him buy his first investment property.

"He instructed him to not sign up for any credit cards in college, upon graduating get a job and save all of his money for three years. While many of his friends were going for the short pass of buying new cars, clothes, cell phones, etc, his son was saving for the big throw- that is investing. After three years, he saved his money and bought an apartment building. He moved in for several years and then used the equity to buy his first home."

"Equity, what's that?"

"I will explain it in a way you can understand. His son bought his apartment for $100,000 and stayed in it for two years. After the two years, people were trying to by it from him for $200,000."

LT did not understand, so he asked, "How did his apartment building go from $100,000 to $200,000 in just three years?"

"Great question LT. In the business world we call it appreciation. I know is sounds like a big word but it isn't. Appreciation simply means that over time things increase in value or worth. Let me give you several illustrations.

"First, we will use an illustration about a guy who is the star of the football team in his senior year in college. During the first half of the season, his stats aren't that earthshaking. However, his team still goes undefeated and plays for the national championship. He has an outstanding game, they win, and on top of that, he is named MVP. What would you think his chances are of being the first round draft-pick?"

"It would be guaranteed," replied LT.

"Are you saying his stocks went up or appreciated as his performance got better?"

"Exactly!"

"Now here's the second illustration. Do you own baseball cards?

"Yes."

"Okay, which one costs you the most?"

"My Hank Aaron card."

"How much did you pay for it?"

"Seven years ago, my day paid $100."

"Today, how much is worth to you?"

"A lot more than $100."

"LT, are you saying the card is worth more today than it was seven years ago?"

LT jumped up and started dancing around his chair.

Mr. Daniels asked, "What's wrong with you?"

He pointed at Mr. Daniels and said, "My mind just connected another dot."

"What do you mean LT?"

"You want me to save my money and buy things that pay me interest. Take the interest money and purchase an apartment building. And like winning the championship or baseball cards, my property will appreciate or become worth more over time."

"Mr. Daniels jumped up and started dancing with LT shouting, "That's right!"

After a couple of minutes Mr. Daniels said, "Okay LT, let's sit down so I can catch my breath. Plus, I have two more points to share. Remember my friends' son's property that he bought for $100,000 but people wanted to buy it for $200,000?"

"Yes."

"Well he sold it for $200,000. Since he sold it for $100,000 more than he bought it for, the government wanted to tax him on the extra $100,000 he made on the deal."

"That's not fair that the government can tax him on the money he made," replied LT.

"It's okay. They need the money for police, firemen, road repair and so forth. But the point is, my friend's son never paid the taxes because he understood how to use the 1031 tax exchange and deferred paying capital gains."

"What in the world did you just say Mr. Daniels?"

"Let's use your baseball card to make this illustration. You said your card was worth more today then when your father bought it seven years ago, correct?"

"Yes"

"Now suppose you sold the card for $200 to a collectable store."

"Wow, I would get a profit of $100."

"But wait LT, there is more. That extra $100 you made from selling your card will be taxed $25, let's call it capital gain taxes?"

"I got it."

"Now, what if they said that you did not have to pay the $25 capital gains taxes right now if you purchased a card worth $300, would that interest you?"

"Of course, because that card would be worth more overtime."

"Good answer. Instead of paying taxes on your card, you defer or put off paying taxes since you gave them more business. Like your $300 card, my friend's son deferred paying capital gains taxes using what many investors know as the 1031 tax exchange. In plain English, the 1031 tax exchange is a program that the government permits a person the right to defer their capital gains taxes if they purchase a higher piece of property."

"Wow, I never knew that! Why isn't everyone else doing what he did?"

"LT, people are losing in life because they are playing it safe. They buy toys for the appearance of having money, but in reality, they are struggling. What I am teaching you is to think like a champion, strategize and go for it. Even football teams have to try something big by throwing a Hail Mary. Now do you understand why I said people are selfish?"

"Yes, they think only about today instead of going for the big play."

Mr. Daniels displayed a half smile to LT's comments. "Remember, always to take good care of that pen because one day you will need it. One last thing; I have an assignment for you. Sometime during the week, I want you to ask at least five adults about capital gains and the 1031 tax exchange and tell me what they say."

LT agreed to the assignment.

Man Point or Question:
What do you remember about the 1031 tax exchange program?

Man Point or Question:
How do Capital Gains work?

Man Point or Question:
What does appreciation mean?

Investing Is Like a Three Pointer

During the entire week leading up to his Saturday's meeting, LT did exactly what Mr. Daniels had instructed him. He asked teachers, storeowners and even some of his friend's parents. To his amazement, not one person knew about the 1031 tax exchange. Only several of them were familiar with capital gains.

After his question and answer session, he went home and into his room for quiet time. While sitting on his bed, he thought about how Mr. Daniels was so kind to share this information with him.

After a couple of minutes of bathing himself in deep thought, LT got up and decided to do his own experiment. He went over to one of his friend's house. When he got there, most of his friends were in the back yard shooting hoops.

One his friends named Billy said, "Look who's here, Mr. stingy."

LT did not respond but sat there listening to their conversation, waiting for his chance to ask a question. As another friend was ending his comments, LT saw the door of opportunity open and immediately asked, "What are you guys going to do after high school?"

Other than the smart remarks by several, no one wanted to talk about it. So LT asked another question, "How will you make money after college?" Again they made didactic comments to his questions. Soon LT decided to leave. As he approached Mr. Daniels' house, Mr. Daniels saw LT and could tell that something was bothering him.

He asked, "What's' wrong?"

LT responded, "I talked to a number of people and they do not want to talk about money. My friends are more interested in basketball and playing their PS2s."

"I am teaching you how a man must take care of his business. Everyone is not interested in this topic so don't take it personal. As a young man, you are learning what most adults wish someone taught them when they were your age. Like Jordan, you are learning how to be the best at your game- that is the financial game.

After few minutes Mr. Daniels started his lesson.

"Today I am going to share with you about stock options. Many people have never heard about options."

"What is an option?" asked LT.

"In the financial world, options are like three pointers; it's a long shot but when you make it, it feels great! Many players try three pointers but few can make them. But with practice and tricks of the trade, you will increase your percentage and separate yourself from the average three-point shooter. The option game is no different. They can be tricky to understand so I want to put your thinking cap on. Let's go back to your Hank Aaron trading card.

"Suppose you were thinking about selling your card and instead of going through the collectable store, you choose to offer all your friends a chance to buy it. Now, one of your friends came up to you and offered let's say, $250. You agreed to the price but told him he has no obligation to buy it, but the deal was only good for thirty days. In this case you gave him the option to buy it. Now suppose he went out in the neighborhood and tried to sell that trading card without ever owning it."

"No way, he does not own it."

"No, he doesn't own it, but he has the option to buy it within 30 days. Your friend has the option to buy, or what investors refer to as a 'call', your Hank Aaron card for $250. If he sold it or what investors call a 'put', for $350, he would make a $100 profit. The contract between you and your friend give him the right to buy ('call') and sell ('put') and you the right to sell the option but for a limited time. Now I want to talk to you about hedging. Your friend hedged your card."

"What is hedging?" asked LT.

"Imagine, two minutes left in the game and your team is up by one point. Your team member throws you the ball. What will you do?"

LT said, "That's a no brainer; protect the ball."

"Great answer. In like manner, when your friend is hedging, he is protecting his investment, that is the Hank Aaron trading card. So since you offered him the option to buy, he was able to sell the card as if it were his. In the adult world, investors use this sample principle everyday. Over the years, investors have made millions buying and selling options.

"When you become a man and get a job, your company will ask you to buy stock, their stock. Stocks are tools companies used to get investors to put money in their company and pay your dividends or interest for using your money.

"When you start buying or selling stock options, you are working on the front-end and that is where you will make money. However, buying regular stock or what we call the back-end, is what we call the leftovers.

"In other words, the front-end is for the end crowd, the movers and shakers. Since stocks are more valuable at the front-end because investors are taking a chance with their company, companies are willing to pay more.

"On the flip side, the back-end is stocks being offered everyday on the market. However, the back-end isn't where the real money is being made. LT, I started my first investment for $7.95. Today it is worth a lot, so you hold on to your $25 dollars."

That statement made LT feel like he just hit a nine-footer because now he was hearing how to get in the investment game.

"Remember I told you about interest?"

"Yes, how could I forget the part where I get paid?"

"Well, stocks pay dividends or something similar to interest. So when you start investing, invest at the front-end, not the back-end. There is so much more to this topic of options, so I encourage you to do some personal research online or at the library. So far, what do you think about options?"

He ruminated on his words, and then said, "I did not know there was so much to making money. When I asked, I thought you would tell me to go get a job or something."

Mr. Daniels appreciated his forthrightness and replied, "I haven't told you half of the story. We have so much more to talk about.

It is very important to learn about money at a young age. The sooner you learn, the easier it is to develop good spending habits. Like in golf, bad habits are difficult to get rid of.

"There are many men struggling financially because no one told them about money when they were young. Now they suffer or try to figure it out on their own. Today, the tenor of society is not thinking about the future, but rather the here and now. People want money quick and easy.

"As a man, you will have responsibilities concerning your family therefore, learning about money will get you ahead of the ball game and hit the three pointer every time."

With a humble look on his face, LT said, "Thank you for helping me to learn."

Man Point or Question:
How do you think about options?

Man Point or Question:
How are you going to learn more about options?

Man Point or Question:
How do you feel about this book so far?

How to Be a Good Team Player with Your Credit

Before going over to Mr. Daniels, LT's parents asked him what he had been doing on Saturdays for the past few weeks. He replied, "I have been hanging out with Mr. Daniels and we have been talking about life." His mother told him that was nice. His father asked, "What have you been talking about?" He replied, "Money. Mr. Daniels has been teaching me about various things about money. After a few minutes of talking with his parents, it was time for him to leave.

LT reached Mr. Daniel's house feeling much better that he had a chance to talk to his parents. When he walked up to the house, his mentor wasn't in the yard as usual. LT called out and Mr. Daniels responded back and said he was in the garage and told him to come in.

He went in and was amazed by the mess on Mr. Daniels garage floor. There were stacks of papers and credit cards. "What is this?" asked LT.

"This is your class for the day. Today we are going to talk about credit. When we first began our talks, I mentioned that adults like to buy pricey toys."

"Yes, I remember."

"Well, those pricey toys can become a problem if a person doesn't take care of their financial business."

"Why is credit so important?" asked LT.

"It is important because credit is the only way companies can see how responsible you are. In other words, credit is a person's report card."

"Report card; I don't get that."

"Here is an illustration. One day a friend comes to you and asks to borrow your $25-"

"No way. I worked too hard for my money."

"Banks feel the same way. They work too hard for their money and they want to protect it like you. Now, for the sake of this conversation, you loan him the money."

"Okay."

"After several weeks he did not pay you like he said he would. Plus, he has not returned any of your phone calls. How do you feel about that?"

"We would not be friends anymore and I would never loan him any money again."

"Exactly," said Mr. Daniels. "For instance, banks and car dealerships judge us by how we pay our bills. If a man cannot keep his word when he signed the contract he cannot be trusted. Bad credit is like having a star player who never keeps up his end of the contract. When he signed the contract, he was given a bonus and endorsements. However, he hardly attends practice and when he does; he gives less than 100%. How would you feel about a player like this during a game and your team needed someone to make a basket and he couldn't deliver?"

"Trade him because he's not a man of his word. I would not want him on my team," said LT.

"Banks, credit card companies and other lending institutions feel the same way. They don't want people on their team who do not hold up their end of the contract. When signing, that player is agreeing to the rules of the team. In like manner, when a person asks for credit they are agreeing to the rules on the contract.

"A man's word is the most important thing he has. The moment he signs a contract, his word is put to the test. It's how they pay their bills that determine their value to the team. If you are paying your bills on or before time, you will receive a high score. However, if you are paying your bills late, your score will be much lower.

"LT, do you remember the movie 'Remember the Titans?'"

"Yes, it is one of my favorites."

"Do you recall two players talking and the captain told the other players that they were only thinking about themselves?"

"Yes, what the other player said to the captain changed the course of the team."

"That's right. Attitude reflects leadership. Credit is the same way. A person with good credit is a leader in the financial game while the person with bad credit is constantly being penalized or cut from the team. They both reflect the attitude of the person.

"Instead of banks just giving away money to everyone that asks, they run what is called a credit check or a financial grade. As an illustration, if a person buys a house, the bank will look at them as an A, B, or C paper."

"A, B or C paper, what's that?" LT asked with a curious look.

"A-paper means a person is paying their bills on time and can be trusted. B-paper is a person who also has good paying habits but has paid late on occasion. However, C paper is the worse of the three. I know in school a 'C' means average, but in the business world, it is like receiving an F grade. In other words, that person is high risk.

"In the adult world, credit is very important. The higher your FICO score, the less you have to pay for borrowing money. However, the lower your score, the more money it will cost to borrow. I apologize, LT. Let me explain. FICO is an acronym for Fair Isaac Company. It is a system that scores adults on how they handle their financial affairs. The name comes from the company that created the system of scoring.

"A FICO score is similar to your grading scale in school. If any adult pays his bills on time, they receive a high score. On the flip side, paying bills late or not paying them at all causes them to receive a bad grade. Here is how a financial report card or FICO score would look like in the adult world.

680-Above - A
620-679-Alt A
580-619 – B
530-579 – C
500-530 – D
Below 499 – F"

"Are you telling me that adults, even after they graduated from school still receive a report card?"

"Yes, LT. Many times adults think they are better than the system in paying their bill late. But I want you to know, like sports, no one wants a bad team player on their team."

LT then asked, "How do they determine the score?"

"One, a person's payment history determines their score, whether they pay their bills or time or late? Another way a score is determined is by a person's outstanding debts. In other words, how much do they owe other people? Thirdly, a person's length of credit history or how long they have had credit with a company. These are just several ways FICO scores are determined.

"One more point. A person with a low score will have to pay more money that those with a higher score just to play on the team. For instance, I know a gentleman that had a D FICO score lower than 610. As a result of his low score, the bank penalized him by charging him more money to borrow their money."

"How much did they charge?"

"Forgive me if I shock you with the answer. He paid $12,000 more for a car that sold for $22,000."

"Are you saying he paid $34,000 for a car that cost $22,000?"

"Yes. He was penalized for paying his bills late."

"Talking about flag on the play. Wow, I did not know the adult world was so complicated? You guys have so many rules."

Mr. Daniels replied, "Like sports, there are guiding principles that a player must agree to and if they do not keep their side of the contract, they will get cut or be penalized."

"What can I do to help myself not get cut or penalized?"

Mr. Daniels said, "I like your attitude. You are thinking like a team player and not a showboat. Here are several things you can do. One, when using credit cards, make sure you have the money in the bank so when the bill is due; you can pay the entire bill off. Two, never and I mean never co-sign for anyone. Three, pay your bills on time. Four, never have more than one credit card at a time. Five, save at least three to six months of the amount of your monthly bills. Place it in a special savings account and never touch it except to pay the bill it has been earmarked for."

"I have really learned so much today about how to be a team player with your credit. This was a good lesson and I have a lot to think about in order to be a team player in the real world," concluded LT.

Man Point or Question:
What do you think about the financial report?

Man Point or Question:
What are you going to do to help your credit score when you get in the financial game?

Man Point or Question:
What do you think about people who don't hold up their end of the contract?

Buying Your First House

Mr. Daniels began his seventh lesson on instructing LT on how to buy his first home. "Make sure you purchase your first home before your twenty sixth birthday."

"Why twenty-six?" LT asked.

"I want you to get ahead of the ball game. While many of your friends are spending their money on fun stuff, you must set your life up first, and then the fun things will come your way. Let me give you an illustration. I am sure you are familiar with Tiger Woods."

"You would have to have your head in the sand not to know who he is."

"LT, today he travels around the globe and his face is known world-wide. He has all the money he will ever need and sponsors are still lining up to give him more."

LT interjected, "He just got lucky didn't he?"

"No way, he earned everything. While many young men enjoyed life, Tiger was at the driving range perfecting his shot. I am sure he thought about taking a break to hang out with the guys, but he didn't. Day after day, he stayed focus on his dream of becoming the best golfer he could be. Tiger spent the money and gave up time while his friends enjoyed life."

"Didn't his father help him?" LT asked with passion.

"He would never have been where he is today without his parents. When I looked at him golfing, I see precision. How did he get that way? Practice. He delayed his gratification and now he is enjoying the benefits."

Unclear, LT asked, "What is delayed gratification?"

"It is when a person holds off on smaller things immediately for something bigger in the future."

"I get it. He worked in advance and now he's reaping the benefits. Other sport figures like Magic Johnson, Phil Mickelson, Michael Jordan, Venus and Serena Williams, Lindsay Davenport, Deion Sanders, Joe Montana, etc., delayed gratification by practicing while others enjoyed life and now they are living the fun life."

"That is correct." Mr. Daniels said. "Like all these great athletes, I want to encourage you to apply the delayed gratification principle and purchase your first home early in the life. There are so many young men that don't know to get in the financial game early, instead making their move late in life. Do you know of any young man in his thirties or forties still living with his parents?"

"Yes. I thought it was okay."

"No, LT it is not okay. That is why I am teaching you on how to buy your home and bring honor to your parents, not shame."

"So how do I purchase my first home?"

"Every opportunity you have, save-to-invest. Don't spend it on cars, cell phones, etc. Let your savings build up during high school and college. The money you save will one day be used to purchase a home. With that being said, I am going to help you get ahead in the real estate game. Here are few simple points for your to-do-list when purchasing your first home.

1. **Check your credit history**. When you become an adult, pay your bills on time. Like stated earlier, lending institutions want to know your financial grade. Bank and other leading institutions will use the three major credit bureaus to get your financial report card. They are Experiean, Equifax and TransUnion. The higher your FICO score, the lower amount of money the banks will charge to use their money. Why? The banks trust those with a good financial report card.

2. **Make sure you have a budget**. LT, your finances must be in order. To qualify, your income should be seventy percent and your monthly expenses thirty five percent. In other words, if your monthly salary is $5,000, banks will make sure that your monthly expense isn't above $1,750. Why, they want to know that you can make your loan payment. Before getting a loan, throw all of your debt over board: the lighter your debt, the easier it will be to get a good loan.

3. **Location, location, location**. Where you buy your house is probably the most important part. For instance, if you purchase a nice home in a depressed neighborhood it would appreciate very little. However, if you purchase a run down house in a thriving community, your home would increase in value.

4. **Pay attention to the fees**. When purchasing a home everyone will try to put his or her hands in your pocket. How? By charging high fees. Before signing any paper work, check and cross check their fees. If you do not understand the contract, ask a friend, family members or someone you respect, their judgment for advice.

5. **Chose the right Realtor**. Having a good realtor is very important. Ask around and listen for the name that everyone is talking about. Also, interview several before committing yourself. The average realtors charges about 1.5% to represent you. Make sure you have someone with you and do not sign anything until it's been reviewed.

6. **Compare the price**. Check the value of the home you are interest in with others within a ten miles radius of the neighborhood. When you bid on the home, start slightly lower than what is being asked. Your realtor will help with this. You should expect the selling to counter at least once or twice.

7. **Get the house inspected**. After you become the owner of the house, you assume everything the house has to offer. Hire a professional company to inspect your home before you sign the contract. If you are dealing with a professional company, you will receive a book about the inspection, both pros and cons.

What do you think about that LT?"

"I really enjoy your teaching. Today this information doesn't mean much, but one day I will need it. I guess if I want to be like Tiger in the financial game, I have a lot of homework to do."

Man Point or Question:
When you become an adult, how do you plan on getting your first home?

Man Point or Question:
What are you doing today that is helping or hindering you from purchasing your first home?

Education Attracts Money

"LT, this is our last class. I would like to close it on this note. If you do anything, go to college and get your degree."

"I know, my parents tell me that everyday. They said, 'Go to college, you will make more money.'"

Mr. Daniels said, "They are giving you great advice. Some years ago, a person could get a great job without having a degree. But today, if a young man enters the job market unprepared, they will find it difficult to get ahead."

"What about the athletes?" LT asked.

"Some of them are an exception to the rule. On that same thought, many of them have degrees. For instance, are you familiar with Jerry Rice?"

"Yes, he is the best receiver of all times."

"To shay, but did you know he graduated college?"

"No, I pay more attention to him on the field than off.

"What about Bret Farve, do you know him."

"Yes, he is a great quarterback. I guess he has a degree also."

"Such players as Jim Brown, Joe Montana, Joe Namath, Eric Dickerson, Bo Jackson, Magic Johnson, Larry Bird, and the list goes on have earned their degrees. These men used their God-given ability to get a degree and now they are using it in the business world."

Mr. Daniels closed his meeting with one last request, "Promise me that you will get a degree and use what I have shared with you to help others. I want to leave you with a financial benchmark for life. These are guidelines that will help you get a good financial start in life. You are not obligated to any thing, but I want to offer them as a gift.

Age 15 – 17
1. Focus on graduating from high school
2. Join SAT study groups and tutoring
3. Enroll in a college before graduating high school

Age 18-21
1. Don't sign for credit cards while in college
2. Get a part time job and save
3. Buy your cars with cash, no payment

Age 22 or 24
1. You should have graduated college with your BA degree.
2. I strongly encourage you to consider earning your Masters degree (optional)

Age 25-27
1. Work on building your credit 750 and higher
2. Purchase your first home
3. Start a college fund for your kids

Age 27 – 40
1. Place a minimum of fifteen percent of your earnings for retirement (Roth Ira, Mutual funds)
2. Seek out the advice of a financial planner
3. Invest in Real estate property."

LT liked the road map Mr. Daniels provided. He accepted the challenge and the two departed their ways. Wait, the story doesn't end here.

At sixteen, LT attended workshops after school to prepare for his college SATs. Each day, his friends played video games or shot hoops, but he worked hard on his academics. When he graduated from high school, he was top of the class.

During his second year in college, LT used the story from Mr. Daniels friend's son as motivation to purchase an apartment building from his student loan and make $35,000. He used this money to leverage for more property plus pay off his student loan. He graduated college with high honors and $50,000 in the bank.

Ten years after college, LT had become a millionaire many times over. He followed much of the advice of Mr. Daniels. One day LT was at home with his wife and kids and received a letter from a carrier. The letter stated that Mr. Daniels had passed away and he was needed to attend a meeting concerning his affairs. The letter reminded LT to make sure he brought the pen that Mr. Daniels gave him.

LT, his wife, kids and parents all entered the room where the meeting would be conducted. Unbeknown to LT, the meeting he was attending was the reading of his wishes after he passed. The attorney in charge asked him if brought the pen as instructed and he replied, "Yes."

As the attorney read Mr. Daniels wishes, LT's heart was beating like at drum at a rock concert. He had left some of his money to various churches, charities and community programs. However when they got to LT, what he heard, he could not believe.

The man that taught a sixteen-year-old, green behind the ears boy, about money and who his neighbors called stingy were richer than anyone could imagine. His estate was worth more than $400 millions dollars. He had investment property in fifteen states; own multiple businesses and a host of investments.

The attorney asked LT for the pen. He reached in his coat pocket and set it on the table. He told LT that Mr. Daniels did not have any children and had no relatives to will his money to. Therefore, LT was awarded $350 million dollars for just spending ten weeks with an old guy that needed a friend. The reason for the pen, LT would need it to sign the contract.

His entire family just sat there for minutes in disbelief. In just one day, LT went from a multi millionaire to having more money than he would ever need in his life.

Man Point or Question:
What do you think of the story about LT and Mr. Daniels?

Man Point or Question:
What is your plan after you graduate college?

CHAPTER 3 | Solid Men Standing Strong

What Is A Man?

Greg and his friends constantly sat around and discussed many things. Their favorite topic was sports. Greg and John were seventeen and Doug was eighteen. One day they talked about the subject of being a man. Doug believed a man was the head of the house and women should respect that. John mirrored Doug's conviction but expressed how women's place was in the home, not the work place.

However, Greg did not share their myopic viewpoint. Although he did not have the answer, he knew it wasn't commanding a family like military troops. He encouraged his friends to join him in a conversation with his uncle, Butch. Greg came from a single parent home, but respected his uncle very much because he was always honest and gave good advice.

Greg's aunt and uncle had been married for twenty years. He was well respected in the community because of his work with the youth basketball and baseball leagues.

When Greg and his friends approached the house, they could see through the screen door that he was hard at work, watching his sport channel. Greg walked in and asked if he could resolve a difference of opinion concerning the topic of manhood.

His uncle asked, "What is the problem?"

Doug jump in and asked, "Don't you believe a man is the head of the house?"

"Of course he is."

"I told you." Proudly Doug echoed.

"Wait Doug, there is more to being a man than being king. Let me asked a question. What is a man, John?"

"Like Doug said, the man is the head; he's the general. Also, the women's place is in the home."

While John was expressing his opinion, Greg's aunt, Stephanie, was walking through the room and overheard their conversation.

Butch asked his wife to join the conversation. "Where did you get that description from John?" asked Butch.

"My brother."

Greg and Doug broke out in laughter. They laughed to the point of tears and fell back in their chair holding their stomach. Butch and his wife did not understand the laughter and asked, "What's so funny?"

Greg said, "His brother is twenty four years old, divorced three times, doesn't have a job and sits at home all day and plays his video games."

Doug said, "No way; he's not a man. He's the laughing stock of the community."

To stop the bleeding and help pick up John's wounded spirit Butch stepped in and asked his wife, Stephanie to interject. She said, "Many young men like you have the wrong concept of manhood. As a woman, we are not interested in someone that slams their hand and demands respect. Nor are we interested in someone that tries to beat us into submission."

"Why do you say that, Aunt Stephanie?" asked Greg.

"Because your uncle tried it and it did not work."

After hearing her words, all three-boys looked at Butch in amazement.

"Don't look shocked; she is telling the truth. I tried that and other things before finding out my role as a man. I learned from bad examples in the street and work. Their bad advice almost cost me my married."

Greg was shocked to hear his uncle and aunt had cracks in their life. He said, "I never knew that you had problems, everything looked so peaceful."

Butch said, "Greg, every married couple has skeletons locked up in a closet somewhere. Let me tell you our experience. Before you were born Greg, I had the same beliefs as John. I thought your aunt should know her place. She should not speak until unto spoken to. I stayed at home, watched sports while she worked. Boy was I wrong. When Stephanie came home from work, I demanded she cook me dinner."

"If you were home all day, why did you not prepare your own food?" asked John.

"I believed it was her place, not mine. Also, I believed that my wife's check belonged to me and she should not spend any money without permission."

"Wait a minute, responded Doug. You did not have a job. You watched TV while your wife worked and thought her check belonged to you?"

"Correct. Today it sounds dumb, but I thought like that. Whenever we attended a social gathering, I told her what to wear. I wanted to control her every move. Once I saw my wife in the store wearing something without my approval, I snatched her out of line and took her home. The way I treated my wife still hurts as I think about it. Several guys in the street told me that my wife should know her place and if she did not, I should beat it into her."

"Are you telling me that you beat Aunt Stephanie?"

"Yes. I only did it once, but that was all it took to break the dam and let the flood of trouble splash down. I hit her so hard that she had to be taken to the hospital. I fractured her jaw in two places." After hearing that, a hush sound came over the room that a dropped pen could be heard from upstairs.

"After hitting her, I was arrested and that was the beginning of my troubles. It cost me years of counseling and two years in jail. I am not proud about going to jail, but it helped me realize my mistakes. When I got out of jail, I spent several years with my grandfather and he gave me the best advice anyone could have given me."

Curious about his statement Greg asked, "What did he tell you?"

"Being a military man he told me a real general leads his troops into battle. In others words, a real man should lead by example."

"How?" John asked.

"As a husband, I demanded my wife to do what I was not willing to do. She worked while I lay around being lazy. I am not saying that she should not work, but she wasn't the problem, I was. My arrogance blinded me. She paid the bills, while I did not work for two years."

"Two years, Doug said with a little fire in his voice, how could you not work for two years?"

"I was stupid. Today, I never ask my wife to do anything I am not first willing to do myself. It is my responsibility to lead by example, not by force. My grandfather told me that a man never has to make his family obey him if he does what is right. No one wants to follow a tyrant."

Stephanie said, "Today, we have a high respect for Butch. Why? He earned it. Here is something that might shock you young men. A family feels secure when a man is confidant in who he is."

John asked, "What do you mean?"

"Now that my husband is the example in our home, it's not hard to follow him. He knows where he is going and we are happy to take the journey with him."

Butch ended the talk on this note, "Today, young men have no clue what it means to be a man. If you want to be respected, be the role model by leading. I hope what I shared will help you understand how important it is to be an example in your home, not a demanding or immature man like I was."

Man Point or Question:
What do you think about Butch and Stephanie's experience?

Man Point or Question:
What do you think about Butch's grandfather's definition of a man?

Man Point or Question:
What will it take for you to be a positive example?

The Character of a Man

Big Ed was what many would call a seventeen-year-old blue chip player. He stood towers above anyone in the school. His arms were as long as a regular bat and his hands could grip half a basketball and his vertical leap was off the charts.

During basketball season scouts would come from miles just to see this towering athlete display his talent. As he sprinted up the court he had the stride of a stallion. Once in a game, he dunked on over four of his opposing players causing all of them to fall down in complete embarrassment. To them, he represented a nightmare come true.

Big Ed was like Magic Johnson, Kareem Jabar, Michael Jordan, Dr. J, and Larry Bird rolled into one. Like Magic, he could pass the ball under his legs or behind his back without looking or breaking his stride. As Jabar, his hook shot was always on the money. Like Jordan, he could jump from behind the key and slam the ball with authority. As Dr. J, he was blessed with the agility to move just about any where he wanted. Lastly, he could make a three-pointer regardless of who covered him as only Larry Bird could do. Yes, he was one of a kind.

His team never loss a game and won by not less than thirty points. He averaged forty points per game. Big Ed received more awards than any high school player in history and was named the All-American high school player four straight years.

Before his sophomore year many of the major universities was on the recruiting trail. He was offered cars, money, and one recruiter even offered to pay his grandmother's mortgage if he attended their school. After every game, he was rushed by the media in search of that one exclusive interview. One local newspaper superimposed his image next to the empire state building holding a basketball. Like always, he was the center of attention.

Academically, he had a 4.3 GPA and scored top of his class on the SATs. Most of his classes were honors and he was loved by his teachers and fellow students. Yet, beneath this magnificent sculpture of a coach's dream, was a boy in search of manhood.

Growing up, Big Ed did not have the luxuries like most kids. His mother passed away at birth and he never met his father. His grandmother raised him and taught him whatever she could about life. He loved her and promised when he became a pro; she would never work another day of her life.

With all his fame, he never forgot his friend Bucky. He wasn't known like Big Ed, but he had a heart of gold. One day Bucky asked, "How does it feel to be a star?"

Big Ed replied, "I really don't care about all that. Now that I'm graduating high school, I am scared."

"Scared? Scared of what?" Bucky asked in shock.

"You have been blessed with a father to teach you about being a man. I need someone to teach me. When people look at me they see only the basketball player, not a young man lost when it comes to life issues."

As they were talking, Mr. Jake, Bucky's father drove up. As he got out of the car he spoke to the boys and Big Ed asked if he would teach him about being a man. He agreed, sat down and talked with them.

Mr. Jake began, "On the court, you dominate other players. Off the court, you must have character. That is, the way you live. Why? You are a role model to others. Many great men have traveled the road you're about take, but without success. Yes, they made their millions but their life off the court was a complete shame.

"He isn't a man if he is not willing to stand for what is right. Anyone can agree with the majority when they are wrong, but it takes character to stand for what is right. Your integrity must precede your athletic ability. In other words, respect your reputation more than playing basketball."

"Mr. Jake, it's hard when all those girls are throwing themselves at me or the media says great things about me."

"I know it is, but that is where the men are separated from the boys. My father taught me years ago and I have taught Bucky the same, real men have character.

"I know many men in their forties still acting like boys. Their words aren't worth anything. They make lots of money, but their family doesn't respect them. If you ever wanted to know who is a real a man, look at his family. When he speaks on truth, see if you can see a glow of confidence on their face or do they wear the face of 'I wish he'd stop lying to people' look."

"Mr. Jake, how do you know so much?"

"A man taught me like I am teaching you and Bucky."

Big Ed said, "For years my grandmother has taught me about doing the right thing, but it seems different coming from you."

"She taught you very well, but only a man can make another man. Now guys, how does it feel to go to school having to walk through a metal detector?"

Bucky said, "Like we are prisoners."

"You might not believe it but there was a time that did not exist, said Mr. Jake. In fact, our parents were informed if we did anything wrong. Now many schools have stripped the parental influence away. As a result, kids are policing themselves, violence is up, teen pregnancy is sky rocketing, school campuses have become the 21st century drug house and girls getting abortions is accepted and encouraged to name a few."

"That's true," interjected Big Ed. "I personally know of girls who had numerous abortions and still have sex with multiple partners. But I am still a virgin. Because of who I am on campus, no one bothers me. As far as I know, many of the kids learned about sex from the Internet and rap music."

Mr. Jake said, "Character isn't a popular subject. Like training for sports, it requires too much for some people. They make excuses or jokes, but deep inside, they long to do right. If more young men had integrity, schools would not be the playground for wrongdoing. Character is the power to do right and the authority to reject wrong."

Then Mr. Jakes asked several questions. "Big Ed, why are you a starting player but still a virgin?"

"I chose to keep myself until I get married."

"Bucky, why haven't you tried drugs?"

"I'm not interested in hurting myself."

"I want both of you to realize that it took character to make the choices you did. Integrity is a choice and everyone has the right to agree or disagree. It takes nothing to have sex, just find the girl and get your grove on. Likewise, anyone can do drugs, dealers are everywhere and a simple yes can start everything into motion. But to stand firm on your belief in the midst of wrongdoing, that's character in action. As men, we are faced everyday with choices, right or wrong. The choices we make determine the depth of our character."

Man Point or Question:
What do you think about Mr. Jake's definition of character?

Man Point or Question:
What do you feel about character today?

Man Point or Question:
How do you feel about your character?

The Visionary Man

Leonard was sixteen and without a clue of what life was about. To him, if he could just play football, dominos or video games for life, he was okay with that. One day while playing at the recreation center, he saw one of his basketball coaches he had when he was a kid. His name was Jim Malone, but all the kids called him Coach Malone.

As he saw Leonard, he called his name and Leonard ran over to see what he wanted. Coach Malone said, "Leonard, have a seat and tell me how you are doing."

"Fantastic coach. Everything is going fine."

"I can see you have been working on your jump shot."

"O yes. And, do you remember I have that problem driving to the left side?"

"How could I forget?"

"Don't worry, I went to basketball camp and they helped me work the kinks out."

"Where have you decided to go to college?"

"I haven't given it much thought. I've been so busy playing basketball; I have not taken the time."

"What would you like to be doing in five years?"

"I have never thought about it."

"Tell me Leonard, have you talked to your parents about your future?"

"I tried talking to my dad, but he's always too busy. My mom set down with me a couple of times, but she's waiting on my father."

"Why don't you come over and have dinner tonight and we can talk about your life?"

"That sounds great to me. I never want to miss any opportunity to get my grub on."

Around six o'clock Leonard arrived at Coach Malone's home. The dinner was already laid out on the table and Coach and his wife were waiting on him. "Okay young man, go and wash you hands, dinner is ready."

After dinner Coach Malone invited Leonard into his study room. When Leonard walked through the door, he saw trophies, awards, plaques and sport memorabilia. He said, "Wow coach. I didn't know you achieved so much."

Leonard walked around and discovered that Coach Malone accolades consisted of All State high school team and MVP three straight years. He was captain of his college basketball team, All American and runner up for college player of the year to name a few.

"Coach, you must have been really good in your day. How did you accomplish so much?"

"I had a plan."

"A plan? It really must have taken a lot of planning to achieve so much. Most of the guys at the recreation center only dream about accomplishing what you have. Ironically to us, you were just Coach Malone."

Then Coach asked, "What do you plan on doing after college?"

"My brain doesn't think that far in advance."

Coach laughed at Leonard's comments but said, "Seriously, have you thought about your future?"

"Coach, at the center most of the guys dream about making it to the pros."

"I know, but one day you will have to be a man and start making some life decisions."

"Why do I have to think about it right now? I still have time."

"Leonard, I have heard so many guys use that line. Now, many of them are still waiting for their boat to come in. Young man, you have to be realistic because life will not wait for you to wake up and make a decision. It will pass you by. Leonard, do you remember Donald T.?"

"Who could ever forget him? He was the best that ever came out of the center. What college is he playing for now?"

"He's not in school. He is working at a fast food restaurant."

"What happened to his college career? He had the skills."

"We all knew he had the skills, but he did not have a plan. Like you, I talked with him but he did not listen. He tried to ride the coattail of his basketball success, but it failed him. When he arrived at college, there were much better players competing for the same position. He could not handle the pressure of sitting on the bench so he left college. Since he did not have a backup plan he had to accept the first job available. Now, do you remember Jason Smith?"

"Oh yes. We called him baby magic because he could move on the court like Magic Johnson. Don't tell me he's working for a fast food restaurant?"

"In fact, he is. Instead of working there, he owns it. After college he did not get drafted so he opened BM's rib shack."

"That's his restaurant?" Leonard said with excitement. "He has at least five in the city, plus several others throughout other cities."

"That's right. He is a very successful business man. Like Donald T, I talked to Jason about his future. He listened and we devised a plan just in case he did not go pro."

"Okay Coach, I want you to help me with my plan. Where do we start?"

"First, here are several questions I want you to answer -

1. What are you going to do if you don't make the pros? You must have a plan to fall back on. Attending college will give you options.

2. How much money would you like to earn? For instance, if you want to earn $100,000 a year, choose a career that earns that much. Your counselor will help guide you with this.

3. What type of neighborhood would you like to live in? Look in a Real Estate Magazine and find a sample of the house you want for you and your family. Then, take it out and carry it with you to college. Every time you get tired or discouraged, pull it out for motivation. I used this technique to purchase the house you are standing in right now.

4. Other than basketball, what other gifts do you have? If do not know, your high school counselor will help you. There are tests you can take in high school and college to assist you with this.

5. How will you give back to the community? Never forget where you come from. After college come back and encourage the kids like I am doing for you.

"When choosing a college, consider the one that will give you the most bang-for-your-buck. In other words, chose a college that will help you fulfill your dream. Many of your friends will ask you to join them. College is not a place to make friends, you have a plan. Don't get me wrong, you will meet nice people, but don't get so caught up in relationships that you miss your dreams.

"Tomorrow, I want you to go to your high school counselor and ask about career options that fit your degree. Also, ask about upcoming college workshops. Do not worry about taking up their time. That is what they get paid to do.

"Leonard, a man is a visionary. You are the captain of your ship and if you do not have a plan, you will drift for a long time. As a man, we don't sit back and wait for things to fall into place, we plan them. Although we can't guarantee the outcome, we have something to say about what will happen.

"During college, call me. I taught you the game of basketball, as your coach. Now I am going to mentor you and become your life coach."

Man Point or Question:
What do you think about Coach Malone's push for a plan in life?

Man Point or Question:
Do you have a life coach? If not, do you have any suggestions?

Man Point or Question:
What are your plans for the next ten years?

Chapter 4 | Men and Women

Respecting Women

Ben had a very difficult upbringing. As a child, his father had been the tormentor of the home. He would tell everyone they were worthless and he was very abusive. For instance, he beat his wife, Ben's mother; so many times that Ben stopped counting. He could not understand why she never filed charges. Instead, she would go up to her room and cry.

Ben's father was constantly telling his mother how she would never be any thing and that she did not have the brains to make something out of herself. His words were like a snake's venom and slowly it was poisoning his mother's mind. It did not matter if he was intoxicated or had taken his daily cocaine hit; he had rage deep in heart.

Ben's worse experience as a kid came when his parents were arguing upstairs. Like before, he tried to block out the foul language and demeaning comments that rolled out of his father's mouth. During his rage, his father slapped his mother so hard she hit the top of the railing with her head and fell down the stairs.

When the ambulance and the police arrived, his father instructed Ben to say she tripped, hit the railing and fell. Terrified, Ben stuck to the story and his father escaped once again. After the police left, Ben asked, "Why do you hit mom like she is a punching bag? What did she do for you to treat her so bad?"

His father responded, "Ben, many times grownups get in arguments and eventually they work things out. You understand don't you? I love your mother very much, but sometimes I get angry and lose my temper." As Ben grew up, the beatings subsided but never stopped.

When he reached seventeen, he never forgot what his father did. Many of his teachers knew that something bothered him, but they could never figure what was going on in his mind. The only person that brought peace in his life was his girlfriend Sahara Taylor.

They loved taking strolls to the park, sitting by the lake, talking about the future. It was Ben's way of escaping the pain lodged in his heart. They would spend hours after school just listening to the flow of the water and the sound of the wind hitting the trees.

The lake was located just below a grassy hill. It had several types of trees surrounding it and the grass was always cut low. There was a jogging track and several tennis courts to the east of lake. Truly this was a safe haven for Ben.

Sahara lived in the town for four years but missed the simple country life. She came from a small city about three hours away.

Her family was very affectionate to each other. It wasn't hard to notice the love between her parents.

One day Ben and Sahara's was in her backyard talking when she received a phone call on her cell phone. After she got off the phone, he asked about the caller and she told him it was her ex-boyfriend calling about some unfinished business.

To her surprise, Ben started yelling and accusing her of cheating. Sahara asked why he was so upset. Ben shouted, "I gave you my heart and now look what you have done. I knew you were no good!" His voice was so loud that it thundered throughout the back of the house. Her parents got up and came to the window. When they looked out, they saw Ben push their daughter several times.

Sahara's father walked out the door and caught Ben's arm, as he was about to slap her. "Young man, what is your problem?" Mr. Taylor agitatedly asked.

For the first time, Ben realized that he was acting just like his father.

As Ben, Sahara and her parents sat down, Ben started unloading the pain of his childhood. He told them how his father abused his mother and of the anger that has been locked in his heart. He said, "I guess the apple doesn't fall too far from the tree."

Mr. Taylor said, "Your father chose not to respect your mother, but you do not have to repeat his failure."

"All I have ever known is men abusing and controlling women."

"That's your father's belief and actions, not yours. Whenever I get mad at my wife, I walk away. Sometimes it's not good, but I choose that over hitting her. Why? Because I respect her."

"So what can I do to deal with my anger?' Ben asked.

"The first thing you should do is stop. No matter how you feel, calm down and allow yourself the chance get control. People with anger are short sighted, that is, they do not think about the consequences of their action. One of the greatest qualities of being a man is having control of oneself. I heard a speaker once say, 'Men are to be the protectors of women, not the predators.' That is true. You must have control of your emotions and your thoughts.

"Another thing, don't allow things to become bottled up. Say how you feel. Be respectful, but speak up. Maybe you might say something like, 'I don't like it when you hit mom. It makes me feel like you don't love her.' Expressing yourself will help you release the tension. Did you know there are different ways to express your anger?"

Ben answered, "No. What are they?"

"Do you like to write, listen to music, play sports, etc?"

"I enjoy writing."

"Great, write down how you feel. This will allow you to get everything out. As you write, use word pictures."

"What do you mean by word pictures?"

"By word pictures I mean draw a visual image using words. For instance, once in a heated conversation with my wife, I told her my anger felt like a volcano ready to explode and that anytime I could erupt. That simple word picture helped her understand that I reached my boiling point. Word pictures help others get a mental image of how you feel while helping you get free from the anger.

"When you were about to hit my daughter, it wasn't her you were mad at, but your father. A part of being healed from what your father did is to direct your anger towards him, not the innocent. Many times men don't understand their negative actions create anger in their kids.

"Ben, anger is natural, but you must choose the right way to express it. Hitting women isn't it. Holding onto your anger makes you a walking time bomb and it is a matter of time before you go off."

"I know," Ben said. "Sometimes, I feel like I need to hit something just to release the pressure."

"Lastly, a man is accountable for his actions. If he hits a woman he must be willing to accept the consequences of the law. Is it worth it to go to jail?"

"No. My father always had us make up stories about what happened to cover his tracks."

"Again, that was his choice, but you must stand on your own two feet and make your choices as a man."

With these last words Ben went home and took the advice of Mr. Taylor. He wrote a story and asked his parents if they would give them his opinion. When his father finished reading he asked, "Ben, was that story about me?"

"Yes dad."

From reading the story his father finally came to grips that he had a serious problem and agreed to get help.

Man Point or Question:
How do you feel about Ben's father's anger?

Man Point or Question:
What do you think about Ben and how he almost hit Sahara?

Man Point or Question:
How do you control your emotions?

Dating 101

Josh was truly the ladies man. His list of girls could be assembled from the who's who within a twenty-five mile radius. At nineteen, he drove an Escalade with leather interior, surround sounds, TV monitors, and twenty inch rims. He was able to afford such a car because he moonlighted as a DJ. He wore the latest clothes and had every pair of sneakers known to man.

Josh loved to boast about being the godfather of all Mack-daddies. He stood six feet, athletically built, and the girls loved to ride in his car. He had every thing that any young man would dream materially, which made him one of the most narcissists. Josh was no less than a snake in fancy clothes.

One day he and his friend Mark were at the mall. Out of the corner of his eye, he thought he had died and gone to heaven as his eyes captured one of the most beautiful girls he had ever seen. She had long wavy hair, green eyes and the body of a fitness instructor.

Mark said, "Josh, forget about her because you will never get past her dad."

"No problem, I am a master at getting fathers on my side. If there is one thing I know, that is how to deal with daddy. When it comes to rope-a-doping dear old dad, I wrote the book. Give me one meeting and I will have him begging me to be his son-in-law." Josh spoke with his usual arrogance.

Josh walked up to her and introduced himself. She smiled with an innocent look and said, "Camille." She spoke with a soft and intoxicated voice and smelled like a breath of fresh air. For the next hour their conversation bounced back and forth until he finally got her number.

As they walked away, Josh said in a prideful voice, "It's a matter of time before her name will be placed on my sexual trophy case."

On one occasion, Josh drove in her driveway with his music volume at high decimal, pounding on the horn, yelling, "Camille let's go!" As she approached the car her face revealed something was bothering her. Josh asked, "What wrong?" She never answered.

After weeks of talking on the phone, he asked for a date. She agreed but said her parents wanted to meet him. He said, "Next Saturday would be a great time."

As he approached the house Josh thought how this was going to be a walk in the park. Like before he honked his horn to let everyone know he had arrived. But, when he knocked and Camille's father opened the door, Josh's walk in the park didn't look so easy. Camille's dad stood about six-seven and weighed three hundred and eighty pounds.

When he said, "Come in." His voice was deep and sounded like a roaring lion in charge of his jungle. Josh's eyes gripped on him amazed by his stature and for the first time he realized this mission might be impossible. As he walked in the house he saw Camille and her mother sitting in the family room waiting.

Camille's father, Frank Johnson wasted no time, asking a poignant question. "I heard that you are interested in dating my daughter?"

Josh hesitated for a minute and answered, "Yes."

He fired the second question as fast as the first, "Tell us about yourself." Just the tone of his voice and the stare of his eyes made Josh think before answering.

Josh replied, "There isn't much to tell. I've lived in this neighborhood all my life."

For the next hour Frank pounded question after question learning more about this young man interested in his daughter. Then the question of all questions was slapped in Josh's lap, "What do you know about dating my daughter?"

Josh was lost for words. He'd never been asked that before. In fact, a girl's father in the past had never questioned him like Camille's father.

Mr. Johnson sensing Josh's fear said, "If you want to date a man's daughter you must respect his rules. My wife and I love Camille and have great plans for her. Have your father ever taught you about dating and how to respect a man's house?"

He replied, "Not really. He's always too busy to tell me anything. I just try to figure it out when it comes up."

"Well, let me give you your first lesson in dating. First of all, never drive up to a man's house and honk your horn. Get out of your car quietly and ring the doorbell. Honking your horn is disrespectful. Honking your horn tells the young lady and her family she's not worth the time to get out of the car and come to the door. Our daughter has been trained not to respond to anyone who shows such low regard." Josh agreed with a nod.

"Second, whenever you address a man, never respond to him with 'Yeah.' Always say, 'yes sir' or 'no sir.' Your generation may disagree, but a real man looks for signs of respect.

"Thirdly, has any one ever taught you the Ten Commandments of dating?"

"No sir, this is the first I've heard of it."

"No problem young man. I perceive you are not a bad kid, but one day you will be in my seat and I hope you protect your daughter like I do mine."

Mr. Johnson began to share with Josh that dating is about respecting not only the girl, but also her family. Just because a young man is dating a young lady doesn't mean he has rights and privileges, you must earn it. Josh, here are the Ten Commandments of dating a man's daughter:

Commandment #1 - Respect a man's house rules even if you disagree with them.

Commandment #2 – Never hit another's man's daughter.

Commandments #3 – Never disrespect a young lady and her family by honking your horn. Get out of the car, ring the doorbell and don't leave, taking her away without speaking to her family.

Commandment #4 – Respect a man's house by having his daughter home before curfew. You will understand this better when you have a daughter.

Commandment #5 – Never ask a young lady to pay the bill. If you asked for the date, you must be man enough to pay for it.

Commandment #6 – When calling a man's house, don't ask for the young lady without first addressing the person on the phone with a hello or how are you doing?

Commandment #7 – Absolutely, never come in a man's house when he is not home. Even if someone like the mother, daughter, or brother has given permission. Wait until the man comes home.

Commandment #8 – Open and close doors for your date. This may sound corny but a father appreciates it and will ask his daughter about it.

Commandment #9 – Ask a man to date his daughter. Don't take it upon yourself to assume you have the right.

Commandment #10 –Respect a man's daughter and you will receive his trust. Don't assume he trusts you until he tells you. Lastly, remember commandment one through nine.

After Mr. Johnson established the rules, Josh understood that he loved his daughter enough to question Josh's motives for wanting to date Camille. He said, "Mr. Johnson, I want to apologize for breaking your rules. No one's ever taught me." Everyone could tell that Josh was sincere and meant what he said.

Plus, Josh was rather pleased that Mr. Johnson took the time to teach him about respecting a man's home. His only wish was that his father had taught him, but was grateful to Mr. Johnson for stepping in.

Man Point or Question:
What do you think about Frank's Ten Commandments?

Man Point or Question:
How do you respect girls when you date them?

Man Point or Question:
What have you been taught about dating?

Man Point or Question:
How would you like a young man to treat your daughter on a date?

Choosing Your Bride

Joaquin felt it was time for him to get married. He wasn't sure of what to look for in a wife, but was open to learn. While his father was sitting in the family room, Joaquin asked if they could talk. He said, "Dad, if I wanted to get married, how do I find a bride? There are so many girls out there; I do not know where to start."

His father, Mr. Smith said, "Why are you interested in getting married?"

"Several of my friends have gotten married. How do I know when I've found my soul mate?"

"That is funny you ask." Mr. Smith said. "I was just reading an article about the rise of youth marriages and why so many fail."

"Dad, what did it say?"

"One point stressed by the writer was young people get married for the wrong reasons."

"What were some of the wrong reasons?"

"Let me ask a question. What are you looking for in a mate?"

"I guess she has to look good and make me happy," Joaquin responded.

"The writer was correct. He said that younger couples are more interested in what they can get out of the marriage than what they should put into it. And when the well runs dry, they run at nano speed to the courthouse shouting irreconcilable differences.

"Your statement, 'She should look good and make me happy' puts you behind the driver's wheel. That is a place of control. Sounds like the marriage would be more about you."

"I don't get what you mean, dad."

"Joaquin, have you ever thought about what a women looks for in her husband?"

"Not really."

"Like men, women have some basic qualities about their future spouse. They want to know that she will be loved, cared, provided for, and protected. Did you know that communication is important to women? Women are emotional beings and love being expressive. For instance, years ago, I recall an article abut the difference between girls and boys. Girls were very social and spend most of their time talking to each other. On the flip side, boys did not talk as much, instead they made sounds."

"Sounds, what kind of sounds?"

"Boys made sounds like cars, motorcycles, trucks, etc. What do you think is one of the top problems with a marriage? I'll tell you; Communication. Before you look for a wife, check to see if you are a good candidate to be a husband? Before I married your mother, I had a huge list of what a wife should be, however I did not measure up to what I was asking. Let me explain.

"I said she had to be smart, but I was an average student. Also, I wanted her to be in shape and I was fifty pounds over weight. Do you get the picture?"

"Yes dad, but was what you asked wrong?"

"Not really, but I had to be realistic. Now let me ask another question. Are you prepared to take care of another man's daughter?"

"I guess when you put it that way, I have to think about it," Joaquin responded.

"There is a difference between dating and marriage."

"What do you mean?"

"For the most part, dating is fleeting or temporary, but a marriage is a lifetime. Plus, marriage is about taking a risk. No matter what materials you read or tapes you listen to, there is not a guarantee to marriage. All successful marriages are a work in progress. Marriage is about stepping out on faith without any certainty of the outcome."

"I'm not sure about taking the step of marriage if there are no guarantees."

"Joaquin, nothing in life has guarantees, but a least you can do your homework and make sure you are making the right decision for life. There are many points to consider, but here are ten things that will help you in being fair with choosing your bride.

1. **Look for values that are compatible with yours.** One of the most important things about marriage is character. Make sure your morals and values are aligned. In other words, if you believe that lying on your taxes is wrong, but she thinks it's okay, are you willing to live with that knowing what could legally happen?

2. **Don't raise the bar too high**. Be realistic; don't ask what you can't deliver yourself.

3. **Don't judge the book by the cover.** In other words, beauty isn't everything. I don't care if she has the beauty of a model she is more than a sex object for your occasional pleasure. She's a person with feelings.

4. **Make sure both of you have the same interest about family.** Ask how many children she wants. Also, ask how her parents raised her. This will give you great insight about what she really believes.

5. **How well do you and your potential bride connect with each other?** Are you well matched or not? As time goes, you and your spouse must be able to enjoy each other's company.

6. **Why do you want to get married?** If you want to get married because you are alone, hungry for sex, or want someone to take care of you, you're marrying for the wrong reason.

7. **Is this the person you want to spend the rest of your life with?** Unless you are sure, wait. Marriage is a lifetime commitment and something you do not want to take lightly.

8. **How do you feel about long-term relationships?** Again, marriage isn't like dating. After the movies, girlfriends go home. Your wife will go home with you.

9. **How does she respond to her father?** This is very important. A great key to determine your potential spouse is how she interacts with her father or some male figure in her life. All things being equal, if she struggles with her father's authority, there is a great possibility she will grapple with yours. Your grandmother told me this secret.

10. **How will she compliment you spiritually?** I know this might sound insane, but many marriages have fallen as a result of

contradicting spiritual views. In other words, 'Don't get unequally yoked.' People have strong convictions about their spirituality and it will affect your marriage if you and your wife are on different pages."

"Dad, did you use this list before marrying mom?"

"Yes. Like I am sharing with you, my father talked to me about marriage. He stressed that marriage wasn't something to play with. Therefore we should know what we were getting ourselves into. Another strong conviction your grandfather had was no divorce. He told us that we should never bring shame to his name by getting a divorce. If we ever had an argument with our spouse, we were allowed to come home once, but our spouse had to be with us."

"Wow, granddad was pretty strict on you guys."

"To some, yes. However, all eight of my sibling's marriages are thriving. But today's teaching has encouraged young couples to get a divorce faster than a new video game can be released."

"Dad, I guess you are right; sometimes the old way is the better way."

Man Point or Question:
How do you feel about Mr. Smith's list of choosing a bride?

Man Point or Question:
Do you feel marriage is a risk?

Man Point or Question:
Do you think you will be a good husband?

Man Point or Question:
Do you think Joaquin's grandfather's beliefs are old fashioned? Why or Why Not?

Preparing for Marriage

Blair and Chastity had known each other since grade school. They grew up just blocks away and shared the same friends. Blair came from a two-parent home but he and his father did not have a close relationship. His father traveled and when in town, never attended any of Blair's events.

On the other hand, Chastity's mother raised her, her brother and sister. Their family was close knit and shared many things with each other. Although their father lived far away and very seldom came around, it did not stop their love one for the other.

When Blair and Chastity graduated high school they knew it was only a matter of time before they would tie the knot. They both had dreams of going to college but felt marriage should come first. Blair had the dream of owning a Real Estate business while Chastity wanted to be a CPA.

Her close friend Janet told Chastity that she was lucky she hadn't got married nor had kids. Looking puzzled, Chastity asked what she meant by that statement.

She said, "You still have a chance to make something out of yourself. My husband and I have several kids and neither one of us have a good job to support the family. We always talked about how in love we were. We spent many days at the park talking about what our family would be like. Now we are struggling just to make ends meet."

Likewise, one of Blair's friends told him that marriage wasn't like they pictured it would be. He did not prepare for the many problems that came with marriage. He shared how they were not prepared for the financial issues, marital conflict, or parenthood to name a few. Blair could see the frustration on his face as he talked about his life.

"We have been married only two years and now we are talking about divorce."

"Divorce!" Blair shouted. "You and Diane are in your early twenties and have been together for several years, why are you talking about divorce?"

"We rushed into marriage and now we are very unhappy. If we could only turn the clock back, I would have received some type of counseling."

"Why didn't you get counseling?"

"We did not think it was that important. Now I realize it was more lust than love. We were not prepared for something so important." Blair left the conversation questioning the entire issue of marriage.

Several days latter he and Chastity talked about their conversation with their friends. Blair suggested they received pre-marital counseling before making any decision about getting married. She agreed and they scheduled a session with Pastor Alexander from the church in the community.

As they set down with Pastor Alexander, he said, "So you guys are interested in getting married. Why?"

Blair said, "We love each other, but lately many of our friends have been sharing their problems and we don't want to make the same mistakes."

Pastor Alexander responded, "A wise choice. Did you know that more than fifty percent of marriages end in divorce? Looking at each other they turned to the pastor and asked, "Why?"

"There are many reasons, but like your friends have told you, preparation is somewhere on the top. Although pre-marital counseling isn't a guarantee for not getting a divorce, more than seventy percent of those who have received counseling remain married. Unfortunately so many couples jet off to Las Vegas or some drive thru marriage place and tie the knot without knowing what they are getting involved in. Marriage isn't something you just drive thru, say 'I do', and live happily ever after. It's an investment."

"Investment, what do you mean?" Chastity wanted to know.

"First, do either one of you have a good job?"

"Not really." They both replied.

"Where do you plan on living?"

"With my parents until we get on our feet." Blair responded.

"Have you asked your parents?"

"No, I was going to get around to that."

"Blair, your statement lets me know that you are not ready. I am concerned that you are not financially and emotionally ready to take on the responsibility of getting married or raising a family." Those words felt like a locomotive slamming into his chest. Blair wasn't prepared for such truth.

Pastor Alexander said, "I want to ask another question. Why are both of you choosing to do things backwards with something as important as marriage?"

Confused, Blair asked, "What do you mean backwards?" "Neither one of you has a job nor a place to live, so why are you interested in marriage?"

"Because we love each other." Blair spoke thinking he had a great come back.

Pastor Alexander said, "Love doesn't pay the bills, money does. Love will not pay for diapers, the electric bill or any other bill, money answereth all things. I know what I'm sharing sounds hard, but if you don't want to be like your friends, you must get your marriage out of the blocks with a healthy start. For that reason, here is a checklist you will need in place before our next session.

1.   If you are not going to attend college, get some form of education and then get a steady job.
2.   Clear all your personal debts.
3.   Talk openly and write down your differences of raising children.
4.   Get your FICO scores. Work on getting both of your scores above six-hundred and eighty.
5.   Put three to six months of financial reserves in a savings account for emergency protection.
6.   Talk about money such as salary, saving strategies and how you will purchase your first home.
7.   Make a list of goals, date and sign it.
8.   Purchase life insurance to protect the both of you. I know a couple that got married and in the first year the husband died in a car accident. The wife had to sell everything just to pay for his funeral.

9.   Secure a place to stay, such as an apartment.

10.   Make sure your checking account is in order.

11.   Get rid of any old flames and throw away your black book.

12.   Create and sign an abstinence contract.

"One more thing, if and when you decide to get married, keep your wedding cost to a minimum. Instead of presents, request monetary gifts. Also, purchase your furniture with cash. Don't try to be like your parents and have your home fully furnished. Instead of focusing on outfitting your home or apartment, give yours time to work on your marriage relationship. Pay cash for everything in the beginning."

Blair and Chastity were pleased with their first session. Unlike their friends, they had a sound road map before getting married. They both thanked Pastor Alexander and walked out of his office with a greater respect and love for each other.

From that day on, they talked about every thing. Blair accepted the responsibility and put the marriage on hold until the entire checklist was completed. Chastity respected Blair more because he took the counseling serious and accepted his role as a man.

Man Point or Question:

How do you feel about pre-marital counseling?

Man Point or Question:

What do you think about Pastor Alexander's checklist?

Man Point or Question:

How will you prepare for marriage when your time comes?

Man Point or Question:

What are you doing today to prepare for your future?

Celebrate Your Honeymoon

Richie and Ashley were excited about their wedding day. The cake had been ordered and the bride maids and groomsmen had purchased their clothes. Everyone was happy that these two had finally decided to get married.

It had been several years since they graduated high school and both were ready to tie the knot. Ashley's family loved Richie and thought he was very respectable. Likewise, Richie's family adored Ashley and welcomed her into the family.

During their ninth grade year, Richie and Ashley made a vow to remain abstinent until marriage. Many of their friends thought it was ridiculous, but they committed to it anyway. One way they protected their vow was not to date alone. Both agreed that double dating was their best route.

If there were a couple that followed the book, it was Richie and Ashley. Richie purchased the rings a year in advance and secured an apartment about ten miles from their family. Richie had his job secure while Ashley was attending college to get her BA in Real Estate, Law and Finance. Upon her graduation, Richie would enroll in college to obtain his business degree.

Also, they attended a six-week pre-marital counseling session and completed it with flying colors. Each week the pastor was amazed how this young couple was so organized and how strong their love was for each other. At the conclusion, he told them they were the best couple he had ever counseled before. I guess one could say they were the poster children for engaged couples.

Many of the family members came from around the country for the wedding. One of Ashley's cousins in the military named Greg flew from Germany just to be with his favorite cousin. Everyone kept his presence a secret until the night before the wedding. When she saw him and his family standing in the kitchen at the family dinner, her heart felt as if it dropped on the floor, she could not believe her eyes.

One of Richie's best friends that got drafted in the NBA out of high school surprised him by coming. Richie and Jason grew up together and had a very close relationship. He was glad that Jason took time out of his busy schedule to attend his wedding.

Before the wedding, romantic music played in the background as a slide show of Richie and Ashley's life flashed on the big screen. They had twenty-four members in their court and a live band.

Ashley's dress had a long train with sequence that could be seen sparkling from the back of the church. As she walked down the aisle, Richie said to himself how blessed he was to marry such a beautiful person.

Richie chose to sing his vows. Everyone could tell it took all of Ashley's strength to stand as the tears ran down her face as she listened to him. At the end of his singing, Richie had arranged for doves to be released. Everyone could hear the sniffles throughout the church, as most of the women were touched by the ceremony.

Near the end of opening gifts, Ashley's parents had given a gift that meant the world to her; an all expense paid trip to Italy. Why Italy? As a child she told her parents that one-day she wanted to go there. She had pictures posted on her bedroom wall and dreamt about it all the time.

Immediately after the wedding they jumped into the limo and headed to the airport for their honeymoon in Italy. Richie and Ashley were excited about their trip and could not wait to get there. They spent the entire time on the plane talking about what they were going to see.

As he embraced his new wife something happened that no one expected. Richie looked at Ashley and accidentally called her Shelly.

"Shelly? Who in the world is Shelly? And why are you thinking about her on our honeymoon?"

Not sure what to say, Richie knew this night was over. He began to explain that Shelly was a stripper from his bachelor party that his friend Jason threw for him the day before the wedding.

"How could you call a stripper's name on our wedding night?"

"I'm sorry, I messed up." Richie exclaimed. As Richie continued talking, her greatest fears gripped her and she had to know.

In fear of his answer, Ashley asked, "Did you have sex with her?"

Richie tried to avoid answering her question, but finally told her, "Yes."

Ashley's heart was broken. She asked, "Why did you make the vow if you planned on breaking it?"

"I did not plan on breaking it. I got drunk and that is all I remember. When I woke up, she was in the bed with me."

Instead of having a honeymoon worth remembering, Ashley spent the night in tears until she fell asleep. She awoke only to find Richie wasn't in the room. Two hours later, he came in and she could tell that what he had done was bothering him. She asked, "Where have you been?"

"Thinking about what my father taught me." Richie said. "He always told his sons to be men of their word. On the most important day of my life I broke my word to you and it really hurts. He also told me that a man must have character and if he failed, don't run, stand up and face the heat. For the first time in my life, I drank and look at what it cost me. I never knew that one bad decision could cost so much.

"When I left this morning, I went for a walk to clear my head. I told myself to accept whatever decision you make. If you divorce me, I understand and will honor your wishes."

As Ashley listened to him, she found it difficult to get pass the pain of what happened but told him she did not want to divorce him, but felt betrayed.

"I don't know how you feel, but I know it is worse than how I feel." Richie said with a trembling voice.

As I walked around, every thought imaginable flashed through my mind. I promised you a commitment and I had to know what happened, so I called Jason. As I searched my pocket to find his number, I found a card from him.

"What did it say?" Ashley asked. "Jason said that after I got drunk he put me in the bed. He spent the night in the room to make sure nothing happened."

"Why was she in the bed?"

"It was a prank by several of the guys."

"So nothing happened between you and Shelly?"

"According to this card, nothing happened. I still tracked him down and he confirmed that nothing happened. He sat in the chair all night to make sure I protected our abstinence vow. He never agreed to the prank, but apologized for what they did. He had to catch an early flight and catch up with the team and was unable to reach me. So, he put this card in my jacket knowing I would bring it with me. Ashley, my father raised me to be better than this, I only ask that you forgive me."

Man Point or Question:
How do you feel about Richie's decision to drink?

Man Point or Question:
How do you feel about a man keeping his word?

Man Point or Question:
What do you think about the prank by his friend?

Man Point or Question:
How important is your honeymoon to you?

Being the Provider

Jerome and his mother lived a quiet life. She worked several job and he worked part-time at the grocery school after school. He was very interested in going to college to study music but unsure if he would because of his financial situation.

As it got closer to determine where he would go to college, he felt it was time to approach his father for help. He tried several attempts to reach his dad but was unsuccessful. Finally he made contact and went over to his house.

Jerome and his dad sat down and he asked him about school. Jerome told him that school was great but it was time to register for college and he and his mother could not afford it. Jerome said, "Dad, I need your help."

He replied, "Jerome, things are tight right now and I am not in a position to help you go to college.

"How can you not help me? My entire life mom has taken care of me. You have never attended any of my school events and now I want to go to college and still you will not help me."

"Son, things are not going well right now, but one day I will make it up to you."

Jerome responded, "Dad you are living large while mom and I struggle in a two bedroom concrete box. You have two cars and we catch the bus."

"Son, I know we haven't had the best relationship but I will make it up to you." "Why do you keep saying you will make it up to me? I don't need your help one day. I need it now. Don't you feel any sense of being a provider? I never asked to come into this world, but you have chosen to walk away from your responsibility as a father."

After several minutes with no success, Jerome decided it was time to leave. When Jerome got home, his mother could tell he was discouraged by his conversation with his father. Like before, she had to console him. While Jerome and his mother were taking about his conversation with his father, there was a knock at the door. When he opened the door, it was his favorite Uncle Gilbert and Aunt Brenda. He loved his uncle very much because he was the father he didn't really have.

Uncle Gilbert could tell something was wrong and he asked, "Jerome, what's the problem?"

He looked at his mother and she told him it was okay to speak up. "Uncle Gilbert," Jerome said. "I just left my father's house asking for help for college and the only thing he had to say was, "I will make it up to you."

"Jerome, since we were kids, both of my brothers have been that way. As boys, they were not responsible. I love both Justin and Jimmy, but that is the life they have chosen to live."

"Uncle Gilbert, I am confused. What is the role of man as a provider?"

"Nephew, a man's responsibility is to provide for his family; there are no exceptions. My brother, Justin, has chosen to live opposite of what our father taught us."

"Why didn't he listen to Grandpa?"

"The world only knows Jerome, because I don't have a clue what Justin is thinking sometimes."

"So what is a provider?" Jerome asked.

"When Justin, Jimmy and I were about your age, our father sat us down and we knew it was going to be one of his talks. He told us that manhood is very important and that one day each of us would have a family. We were to be responsible in many areas, not just financially."

"What are those areas Granddad talked about?"

"Okay, but you will need to write them down. He wanted us to know that being a provider was more than getting money, it was a lifestyle."

"Lifestyle, I don't get it." Jerome said.

"Listen and see if it makes sense to you. One, provide financially for your family. It is our responsibility to take care of our family, not our wife or a court system. If we made the baby, it was our job as a man to take care it.

"Two, attend your children's events. Go to sporting events, school and community and church. Never let your children grow up by themselves.

"Three, teach your children about money. This was one of the big items on your grandfather's list. Each one of us was taught by him about investing, banking, careers, you name it, he taught us about it.

"Four, tell your wife and kids, you love them everyday. He believed that a man set the tone for the house by what he said and did.

"Five, make sure you touch your wife at least eight times a day."

"Touch your wife eight times a day. Why? Do you mean I have to go around counting to make sure I touched her eight times?"

"The point he was making is touching creates security and trust. If you touch your wife, she will know that you love her.

Six, buy a house for your family and keep in it the family. Your grandfather stressed the importance of leaving assets, not debt for your kids to have once we are gone.

"Okay, here is the one that topped my dad's list, number seven. Place a clause in your will, that all assets could only be owned and managed by your children, not their spouses. He would say, "Protect your bloodline."

"He knew that sometimes people get divorced and try to strip their ex for everything. For that reason, after I leave this earth all my assets will be left for my children. I love their spouses, but I still have to protect the bloodline."

Jerome looked at Aunt Brenda and asked, "How do you feel about this rule?"

"At first, I was angry and thought how selfish. But at my daughter's Becky's divorce hearing, I got the picture."

"Jerome." Uncle Gilbert said. "Becky's ex husband came into the marriage with little to show. And over the years, he never added much financial support to their marriage. But at the hearing, he told the judge how he deserved fifty percent from their marriage. The judge had to throw it out of court because of the clause your grandfather taught me."

"Do you mean the one that says, "Whoever disagrees is automatically disqualified?"

"Yes. Like me, make sure you protect your bloodline. Lastly, number eight, absolutely never hit your wife or abuse your children. As a man, you must protect your wife, even from yourself. That is, as a husband, we don't have right to be abusive. Our wives aren't punching bags that we can release our frustration on."

"Uncle Gilbert, I am so glad you took the time to teach this to me. I didn't know it took so much to be a provider."

"One more thing Jerome, your Aunt Brenda and I have a surprise for you. Do you remember your grandfather told us to keep the property in the family?"

"Yes. I'm glad my cousin Becky will be well taken care of."

"Well, Becky just moved out. We recently helped her purchased her first home and according to my father and your grandfather; I must keep the house in the bloodline. So my wife and I have decided to give it to you."

Jerome was in complete shock.

"And one more thing, your aunt and I have been saving for your college fund. We have an account set up in our name and I will take you and your mother to the bank and have the money setup to be wired to the school of your choice."

Man Point or Question:
What are your thoughts about Jerome's father?

Man Point or Question:
What are your thoughts about Jerome's Uncle Gilbert?

Man Point or Question:
How do you feel about the rules of Jerome's grandfather?

Man Point or Question:
What do you think a provider is?

CHAPTER 5

A Man's Man

Overcoming Peer Pressure

James was a seventeen year old that struggled with friendships. He did not meet all of the qualifications such as wearing the latest fashions or driving a fancy car. His only source of transportation outside of riding with his mother to school was his bicycle.

His fashion taste was like a throw back to prehistoric times. His jeans were old and dingy and half an inch higher than his ankles. His shoes looked like he got it off the five-dollar sales rack.

At his school, if a young man did not wear pricey shoes, he had a better chance of winning the Heisman trophy and being drafted in the NFL all in the same year than getting a date. Truly James' taste in clothes hindered his social life.

Everyday James was the punch-line to every joke. While the girls made fun of his clothes, the boys pushed his buttons to provoke him to fight. Outwardly, he kept his cool, but inside it started to chip away his self-esteem.

One day while talking with his friend, Stanley, James asked, "Why are the girls only interested in the rough guys? Unless you treat her like a dog, they think you're weak."

"Man I have tried to figure that out and for the life of me, I just don't get it."

Although he did not believe in the bad boy image, he knew it was time to change if he wanted to be a part of the in-crowd. So he took money from his savings and purchased a new wardrobe. He bought a pair of Rocawear Jeans and a pair of Jordans to start. When he finished his shopping spree, James had spent a thousand dollars.

On the next day, James awakened with a burst of confidence. He knew that this would be the day that everyone would accept him. Unlike before, James spoke to his family with excitement. His mother asked, "What has come over you?"

He said, "Everyone is going to like me now because of my new clothes." His father watched and knew he was only setting himself up for disappointment. But James could not wait to get school.

As he approached the quad with his new fashion gear, he heard people whispering, is that James? Many of them were amazed at his change. Some of they guys asked him to play dominos with them. Yes, James was fitting in just fine with his new friends.

Later that day, Stanley was shocked to see his change. He asked, "Man why didn't you tell me about your fashion makeover?"

"I don't know. Yesterday something came over me and I decided to take matters into my own hands."

The next day, James wore a different set of clothes. This time when he approached the quad, several girls asked if he could sit with them. This new acceptance went on for a month. James' future was starting to take off.

One day while sitting in the quad with his new friends, James saw Stanley walking by and asked him to come over and join him. Within minutes of him sitting down, several in the group began to make fun of Stanley's clothes. After several minutes, he got up crushed and discouraged because people made fun of him.

When he got home, James sat down in his bedroom thinking about what happened. He thought his new friends would accept Stanley but instead they talked about him so bad he considered withdrawing from school. James asked himself, what have I done?

He thought clothes would get him in the in-crowd but it did not. Like a chameleon, James was lying to himself. The clothes did not make him feel better, he only got accepted because of his new fashion statement, not who he really was.

When James' father came home he saw him sitting on the bed and asked what was wrong. James felt embarrassed but said, "I thought my clothes would get me in the in-crowd, but it only got my friend, Stanley hurt and I feel like a fool."

He asked, "Why did you want to fit in with that group?"

"Dad, you don't understand. Everyday we are talked about and some have tried to get us to fight. After a while a person gets tired and just tries to fit in, just to stop the bleeding."

"I understand, James."

"Dad, how could you understand?"

"Like you, several of my friends tried to fit in with a group. In fact, it was so bad that one of my friends, Tim, committed suicide."

"How did he commit suicide?" James asked.

"Since he could not take the peer pressure any more, he took a gun and shot himself. All of us were devastated about Tim's decision to take his life."

James had never seen his father cry before, but as he talked about Tim, his eyes were very teary. His father was always strong, but the sound of Tim's name must have brought back some painful memories. James' father had lost a friend to peer pressure and did not want his son to experience it.

"We could have helped him, but we did not know the signs of suicide at the time."

"What are the signs?"

"I don't know all of them, but here is what we noticed in Tim's behavior.

- He started running away
- He seem bored or distanced himself from things
- He made statement like "That is my last time," "I can't take it any more," or "Nobody cares about me anymore."
- He was an A student, but started making D's and F's
- Tim had trouble eating and sleeping
- The clincher, he started giving away some his most prized possessions

"James, you have a strong character like me. I have done my best to build your character and instill a positive attitude about life. You don't have an identity crisis, but what about your friend Stanley? See, we did not think much about the wise cracks, but Tim took it personal and today he is dead because nobody knew what to look for. Today Stanley might be depressed, but who knows about tomorrow?"

This was the first time James' father told him about his friend Tim and did not want Stanley or any of his friends to make such a bad decision.

"When Tim killed himself, his mother died a year later of a broken heart. Devastated, his father started drinking just to deal with the pressure. James, suicide is a selfish act that hurts everyone. If people don't like you for who you are, they will never like you if you do what they say. Never try to please people just to fit in. No group is worth losing your personal pride."

"I know now dad. My new clothes taught me that lesson. After the way they treated Stanley, I realized I made a mistake. Also, I see how it is important to love yourself for who you are."

"That's right. James you are one of a kind. You are so special that God made only one of you on the earth. Instead of trying to be like others, be who you were meant to be. Be yourself; love yourself when others don't."

"The very friends that put peer pressure on you are the ones with the identity problem, not you or Stanley. Go tell him you love him and that he is your best friend; while you have a chance."

Man Point or Question:
What do you think about James' decision to try and fit in?

Man Point or Question:
How have you tried to fit in?

Man Point or Question:
How do you feel about peer pressure?

Man Point or Question:
What do you think about Tim's choice to commit suicide?

Man Point or Question:
Have you or any one of your friends thought about suicide?

Eighteen Is Just a Number

When Pete turned eighteen, he promised he would not let anyone tell him what to do. He was a strong willed and very opinionated young man. Pete did not like people telling him what to do nor did he feel it was his responsibility any longer to do the same chores like taking out the trash, washing dishes or cleaning his room that he had been doing since thirteen. Although he felt this way, he never spoke it openly.

As he got closer to his eighteenth birthday his family could see his attitude changing. Many of the things asked of him had a rebuttal or condition attached to it. For example, when his mother asked him to get out of the bed and take out the trash, he shouted, "Why is it my job? Can't anyone else do it?"

Although he had a conflict with his mother, he and his father were like enemies of war. He felt his father was taking advantage of him and he was a man just like him. Pete was like a walking time bomb waiting to explode.

As a high school senior, he talked to many of his friends about his problems at home. Since several of them were experiencing the same thing, they understood how he felt. His friend Jeff said, "The next time your dad tells you what to do, don't act like you are afraid." Then another friend said, "Yeah right. Pete, just let your father know that you are a man now that you have turned eighteen."

Every Friday night many of the guys would hang out the movie theatre until 2:00 a.m. in the morning. Pete hated that he could not join his friends; his curfew was 12:00 midnight. He had spoken to his father about extending the curfew but he always said no.

Pete worked the night shift and got off every night around 10:00 p.m. When he would come home, his father would leave notes of what he wanted him to do before going to bed. Slowly Pete was building up resentment against his dad and wanted out.

One night he was determined to stay out with his friends. When the clock struck twelve, Jeff asked, "Pete don't you have to go home?"

Feeling embarrassed by the question, he said, "I will go home when I feel like it. I am eighteen and my father has to respect that."

When Pete got out of the bed in the morning, neither one of his parents spoke to him. He thought they were just playing the cold treatment on him. Finally, his mother asked if he would take out the trash, but this time Pete did not respond.

During the next two weeks Pete stayed past his curfew. He thought, "Finally, my parents get the message that I am a man." However, when he got home, his father was sitting at the table with a piece of paper. He said, "Pete, have a seat. Your mother and I realize that you are eighteen and feel you are grown. Therefore, we have a contract for you to sign."

"Contract!" He said with anger.

"Why are you giving me a contract?"

"You have announced that you are a man and we want you to start taking on responsibilities like a man. First, you will start paying $400 a month in rent, plus help with the utility bills. Next, we have removed you from the car insurance and your payment of $800 is due by tomorrow. Lastly, we will no longer pay your car note. Your monthly note is $325."

Pete was furious. In the morning, Pete's mother noticed some of his clothes missing and saw a note on the refrigerator. It said, "I've moved out because the contract is unfair and I need to start being my own man."

After several months, his parents heard that Pete was living with family members and friends. Each home that he stayed in called to let them know that he would not accept their house rules. Slowly, Pete was burning bridges. Finally he decided it was time to go to his grandparents.

His grandfather who Pete called, Poppa Joe, asked, "Why have you decided to come stay with us?"

"Poppa Joe, my dad is being very unreasonable and he will not respect that I am a man."

"Why are you trying to get your father to respect you?"

"He tried to make me sign a contract. I am not a boy anymore. Why do I have to sign a contract? I am not seventeen anymore, I am an eighteen year old man."

"Pete, what do you think it means to be a man?"

"A man is someone that is independent and carries his own. Know what I am saying?"

Poppa Joe said, "Not really, but I think you mean a man gets to do what he wants."

"Yes, that is what I mean."

"Pete, the contract your father asked you to sign, what did it say?"

"It stated that I have to pay rent, my car note, and my insurance. How can I do that? I don't make that kind of money."

"But Pete," said Poppa Joe, "I thought you wanted to be your own man. You know what I am saying?"

He laughed and said, "Ok Poppa Joe, where are you going with this?"

"All your father asked was that you start acting like a man. But you took it as a personal attack. Why do you think eighteen make's you a man?"

"I don't know."

"Grandson, manhood isn't about demanding respect from others but asking more out of your self. For instance, being a professional football player is about raising the bar and accepting greater responsibility. It may look like fun on the T.V., but in real life, it's a job. You have to walk into manhood without shining the light on yourself by saying, 'I am man; you must respect me." No, that is what boys do. A man does his job without telling. Believe me, when you finish, others will know.

"The contract your father gave you is the same one I gave him. When he was your age, he wanted to be treated like a man and do his own thing. So I gave him a contract to prove his manhood. He signed and fulfilled it. It is now your time.

"One more thing, don't burn the only bridge you have left with your parents. Eat your humble pie and go home." With that being said, Pete decided it was time to mend the fence with his parents.

When Pete got home, he sat down, apologized for his behavior. He explained that being eighteen did not give him the right to be respected, he had to earn it. As he was talking, Pete received a call on his cell phone. It was his friend Charlie.

Charlie called to inform him that Jeff got shot and killed last night hanging out at the movies. Charlie said, "I tried to call you, but your cell phone was off."

Peter said, "I was with my grandparents taking care of personal business. What happened?"

"Jeff decided to stay late and hung out with the wrong guys. A group of boys came up in a car, asked if they were in a gang and before anyone could respond, they started shooting. Several got shot but Jeff was the only one killed."

When Pete got off the phone, he was devastated about the news, turned to his parents and thanked them for not giving up on him.

Man Point or Question:

How do you feel about Pete's attitude with his parents?

Man Point or Question:

What do you think about the contract?

Man Point or Question:

What do you think about what happened to Jeff?

Man Point or Question:

What is the definition of a man?

Blessing the Next Generation

Walter and Mac both grew up in the same neighborhood. As friends, they loved playing basketball, chess, and dreamed of being a professional athlete. They came from a middle class family and were fun loving guys.

Walter was a thinker. Many times he would just sit down and think about life. He loved to read and thought about his future all the time. As graduation was approaching, he wondered which college he would attend. Also he questioned what he would do if he did not make the pros.

On the other hand, Mac just loved life. His motto was, "Live and let live." He did not feel it was necessary to get deep into things, instead enjoy life while you have a chance. Unlike Walter, Mac was sure he would make the pros. He had several scholarship offers and choosing which school he would attend was just a matter of time. Right now, it was fun time.

One Saturday afternoon, Walter and Mac, as usual were at the park playing basketball. Walter asked, "What are your plans after high school?"

"To college and then the pros." Mac responded.

"My father told us never plan ahead because most people don't fulfill their dreams anyway."

Mac asked, "Why are you so worked up about what we are going to do after high school?"

"Look Mac, what if we don't make the pros, then what?"

"Walter, I never think about not making it. Since we were little boys, we wanted to make the pros."

"I know, but if it doesn't happen, we need something to fall back on."

"You see Walter, you think too much. Why don't you relax and just enjoy life? Everything is going to just fall into place as long as you leave it alone."

"I don't believe that. Life isn't about chance; it is what you make it, not a roll of the dice. My parents taught me to plan in advance."

"I know Mac, you told me that before. But how often will we get a chance to be teenagers?"

"Once."

"That's right, so let's enjoy it and let life take care of itself. We have only seven months before graduation and then off to college. That's the plan, ok?"

"Mac, do you plan on having a family?"

"Yes. Like my parents, we are going to live life to the fullest. I want to give my kids the exposure I never had. We are going to take trips around the world."

"Doesn't that take planning Mac? "After I make the pros, money will not be an object."

"Okay Mr. Wise Guy," Mac said. "What are your plans?"

"My parents are teaching me about how to bless the next generation."

Mac looking confused said, "Blessing the next generation, I have never heard of that before."

Walter expounded, "For years they have been saving for my college just in case I did not get a basketball scholarship. My parents put aside money for my future and both took out a million dollar insurance policy to protect me if any thing should ever happen to them."

"Do you mean that if any thing happened to your parents, you would inherit $2 million dollars?"

"That's right. But I'm not looking forward to that. I prefer to have my parents. Plus, they have an investment plan to help me purchase my first home. My dad wanted me to have a good start in life and not struggle like he did. My grandfather worked hard so he could go to college. He never had money but made my father promise to help his children like my grandfather was helping him. My grandfather had a living trust on his house."

"What's a living trust?" Mac asked.

"From what my dad told me, when my grandfather died, my dad would now own the home without going through the court system."

Like my grandfather had planned, when he passed away, my father got the house and all his money. My dad used that money to start investing and now he is doing the same for me. One of my dad's favorite sayings is, "Walter, it is important that you bless the next generation like your grandfather. Don't leave your family in debt; help them get a good start."

Walter's parents were hard working people. His father worked as a Real Estate Broker while his mother worked as a schoolteacher and both had college degrees. They lived a simple life investing their money, and planned Walter's future.

Mac parents also were college graduates. His dad was a principal and his mother worked as an office manager. Unlike Walter's parents, they spent a lot of their money on cars, clothes, and boats to name a few. Because both of them came from a poor background, they promised they would love life and not worry too much.

When Mac's grandparents passed, they left his father with a huge financial burden. His grandfather had more than twenty thousands dollars of debt. Plus they had three loans against their house and since Mac's father could not keep up the payments, it went into foreclosure and eventually, he lost the house.

Upon graduation, Walter's parents gave him a $5,000 saving bond as a down payment on his first home after he graduated college. Mac parents gave him a new BMW fully loaded and $1,000 of play money. They told Mac to do whatever he wanted with the money, it was his to enjoy.

Both Walter and Mac went off to college. Unlike the plan, they did not attend the same school but stayed in touch. Walter decided not to play college ball but pursue the dream of owning a business. Mac made the basketball squad his freshman year, but suffered a career ending knee injury. By a twist of fate, both parents passed way just months apart during Walter and Mac's junior year of college.

When Walter got home, he found the book his father had prepared in the event of his demise. The book included phone numbers of people to call about portions of his business, account numbers and passwords. Since, they made funeral arrangements, Walter did not have to worry about their burial.

Because of the living trust, "Walter was the sole owner the home. Days after the funeral, the insurance company gave him a check for two million dollars. His parents left Walter a huge surprise; their bank account was worth $500 thousand. All of their possessions were paid with cash so he did not have to worry about any debt. Walter's parents had blessed their son to have a great start in life.

Mac's situation was not so pleasing. Like his grandfather, Mac's dad left a huge debt for him to worry about. They did not have an insurance policy or plans for the house. Therefore, Mac had to sell the cars and boats just to pay off their funeral. Because his parents did not leave instructions concerning the house, Mac spent the next few years in and out of court fighting for their home. He was finally awarded the home, but had to sell it just to pay legal fees.

In the end, Mac finished college but did not become a pro as planned. He spent his first ten years after college trying to clean up what his parents left. Mac got married and took on the same mentality of his grandfather and father; he used his money to enjoy life. And the cycle of leaving debt continues in his and his son's life.

Also, Walter received his college degree. With his parent's blessing, he was able to continue his education and eventually received his Ph.D. He got married and like his grandparents and parents before him, continued the plan of blessing his children.

Man Point or Question:
What do you think about Walter's life?

Man Point or Question:
What do you think about Mac's life?

Man Point or Question:
How will you leave a blessing for your children?

The Spiritual Man

Daniel was a very troubled seventeen-year-old young man. A cloud of family problems had shrouded his entire life. His life was a continual pouring of one problem after another. Whenever it seemed he could take a breath of fresh air, another storm cloud would move in.

Daniel's father was very well respected in the corporate world as his career was on the rise. Recently, he had closed one of the biggest sales in his company's history. He had been with the company for only three years and had become the top sales person. However, beneath his wonderful career, he had skeletons in his closet.

Daniel's father was a cocaine addict. His addiction caused his family to move four times in three years. Things had gotten so bad that his father sold all their furniture to buy drugs. Many of his pricey tools also were used as collateral to purchase cocaine. Every time things looked up, his father's chemical dependency would cost him his job.

One day at school Daniel felt he was at the point of breaking. The weight of his father's problem was starting to weigh heavy on his spirit. His school had referred him to a therapist and psychologist, but nothing worked. Daniel had reached the point of deep depression.

He had lost all interest in school and himself. Once a bright young man, now he was on the verge of giving up. Daniel's grades and attendance had fallen. Plus, he seldom changed clothes, bathed himself and had become aloof from other students.

There was a place he could find peace at school, outside the library under the big palm tree. During lunchtime, he would pit his tent under the tree and think about running away and on several times, committing suicide. In the midst of hundreds of kids was a young man soaking in pain.

A fellow student named Earl saw Daniel and called out, "Hey Daniel, what are you doing out here?"

Surprised that Earl knew his name, Daniel responded, "I'm just trying to find some peace on this earth."

"Man, I know what you mean. One day I was searching for peace and did not know where to find it."

"Earl, I don't think peace exist for people like me."

At that time, the bell rang and Earl said, "Meet here tomorrow and we can talk some more. The next day Daniel could not wait to talk to Earl.

As he sat under the tree as usual, Earl came walking up with something in his hand. Daniel asked, "What's that?"

He said, "My life history. As a child, I lived in over thirty-five foster homes. So I kept this diary to write my experiences. Without writing, I don't think I would have survived. Almost in every foster home I was beaten and molested. If I wasn't gang raped by other boys, the leader of the home would take me in their room and rape me. Things had gotten so bad, I tried suicide."

"Suicide?" Daniel replied.

"Yes suicide. After you have been molested like I was, life doesn't mean that much. At one point, I felt like a misused rag doll that people used and then threw to the side."

"Wow, I don't know what to say." Daniel interjected. "How did you get in the foster program?"

"My alcoholic father. He wasn't a bad man, but his addiction got the best of him. One day he and my mother were coming home and like always, he had been drinking. He was driving and got in a car accident that killed my mother and the driver of the other car. He was sentenced to prison and I became a ward of the state." While Daniel listened, he knew Earl could relate to his problem.

Feeling that his problems did not compare to Earl's, Daniel said, "I'm sorry for what happened to you."

"Daniel, you don't need to apologize; you did nothing wrong. My father's drinking problem caused a domino effect that destroyed our family."

"How are you able to talk about it so openly?"

"I found peace and promised that I would help anyone who I saw needed help. For the last months I have been watching you and noticed the same signs in you that I experienced."

Daniel was choked by his words and did everything he could to hold back the tears of pain. The bell rang and Daniel asked Earl if he could come over his house after school and he agreed.

On their way home he continued telling Daniel his story. When they reached his house, Earl asked if he wanted something to drink. Daniel replied, "Sure, I am kind of thirsty talking so much."

As they sat down Earl asked, "What do you know about God?"

"Not much. My parents never talked about religion."

"Remember we talked earlier about finding peace?"

"Yes."

"One night after three boys had raped me, I laid in bed in so much pain, both physical and emotionally. I could not understand why I was being treated so badly. So, while everyone was asleep, I got out of bed, took a knife out of the kitchen and went outside to kill myself. I knew it was wrong, but I could not live another day being someone's rag doll."

Interrupting Daniel said, "Earl, I know how you feel, I have thought about committing suicide many times. My father's cocaine addiction is caving away my will to live. Each time I tried I didn't have the courage to do it." As he was talking, he did not realize that his mother and father were listening to their conversation. Their heart was gripped and eyes flowed with tears as they heard their son talk about suicide, yet they remained silent.

"Daniel, while I was outside, I dropped to my knees in tears, looked into the sky and said, "God if you are real, I need peace. I don't want to be molested or beaten again. While I was talking, an animal startled me as it ran through the backyard."

"Did he answer?" Daniel asked.

"Not that night, but the next day when I came home for school, I found out that I had been adopted by a wonderful family. They raised me like their own and never hit or touched me like everyone else. I know that God answered my prayer. You see Daniel, I found peace in God."

"Earl, I have heard people say that God is for the weak."

"They have the right to say whatever they want. But until a person has experienced what I've experienced, it is only talk, not reality. I will say this Daniel; if God is for weak people, then I accept the title.

"Daniel, have you noticed the violence in our school?"

"I know." Daniel said.

"Kids bring drugs to school and sell it like candy. Our school has been an educational drug house. Have you watched T.V. and seen those kids killing fellow students and teachers?"

"Man, this world is going crazy." Daniel echoed.

"That's right, and the one thing we need is God's peace. But the law tells us that we can't talk about it. When I need help, God helps me. It was people that abused me, not God. So the diary you saw me writing reminds me of where He brought me from and one day I am going to tell the story about His grace and mercy."

As he was talking, Daniel's parents walked out of the house. He could tell they were moved by Earl's story by the tears flowing down their faces. Daniel's father said, "Young man, I want to thank you for sharing your personal testimony and want to know about the peace of God that you talked about. I am tired of living on cocaine and destroying my wife and son's lives. I need peace."

Earl looked at Daniel's father and said, "A gentlemen taught me that a man is the spiritual leader in the home. He explained that my father used alcohol as an escape. It cost him everything. But, you still have a chance to help your family."

Daniel and his parents began embracing each other. His father asked them to forgive him and then to their amazement, Earl was gone. Daniel ran to the front of the house and Earl was not there. The next day Daniel asked other students about a boy called Earl, but no one ever heard of anyone named Earl.

He went to the office and they too did not know of a young man named Earl enrolled. Daniel left the office not knowing for sure what had happened, but knew a miracle had taken place. Daniel's father joined cocaine anonymous. He did not want to lose his second chance at life. Daniel never saw Earl again, but understood how important the spiritual role of the man was in the home.

Man Point or Question:
What do you think of Earl's testimony?

Man Point or Question:
How do you feel about drugs or alcohol?

Man Point or Question:
What do you think about Earl?

The Release of the
Making Wealth Happen
Action Plan

Making Wealth Happen *Action Plan* is the next step of the Wealth Is Possible family. Discover how to get your business off the ground or advance your current business to the next level. Maximize your cash flow and let your money work for you. Implement both offensive and defensive business strategies with proven business tools. This is a jam-packed, entrepreneurial treasure chest. Just ***cut-and-paste*** - it's that **EASY**.

The New Release
of Wealth Is Possible

Wealth Is Possible™ reveals the nuts and bolts in a easy-to-read book on how to make money online, how to start a business with no money down, how to retire and still get paid and how to turn profits into income streams, to name a few.

ADDITIONAL COPIES

of

"Man to Man, *Real Answers About Manhood*"

May Be Ordered From:

VChase Investment Group, LLC
P.O. Box 4613
San, Dimas, CA 91773

ORDER FORM

NAME _____

ADDRESS _____

CITY/ STATE/ZIP _____

ITEM NAME	QTY	PRICE	TOTAL
Man to Man, Real Answers...		15.99	
Wealth Is Possible		15.99	
Making Wealth Happen Action Plan		495.00	

SUB TOTAL		
CA. SALES TAX 8.25%		
SHIPPING		
TOTAL		

ADD $1.75 MINIMUM SHIPPING
$10 - $29.99   ADD $3.50
$30 - UP   ADD $6.50

Thank You For Your Order!

20/20 VISION - HIS IMAGE PUBLISHING, INC.
P.O. Box 14311 • Fremont, CA 94539-1211
Email: hisimage@sbcglobal.net
hisimagepublishing.com